101 PROVEN WAYS TO INCREASE EFFICIENCY AND MAKE MORE MONEY IN LAWN CARE

Practical Tactics to Grow a Better Landscaping Business

PAUL JAMISON

101 Proven Ways to Increase Efficiency

and Make More Money in Lawn Care

Paul Jamison

Copyright © 2022 Paul Jamison

ISBN: 978-0-578-34944-2

www.greenindustrypodcast.com

Dedication

I would like to dedicate this book to my friend Naylor Taliaferro. Years ago I found "The Lawn Care Rookie" on YouTube. Although I was already a few years into my lawn care business at the time, I found "the Rookie's" videos to be quite helpful. He honestly and vulnerably shared his experiences as he was in the early stages of building his lawn care business. I would often leave encouraging comments on his videos and thank him for sharing this information with the world. As time went by, Naylor eventually invited me to be a part of one of his private mastermind groups. That networking opportunity was life-changing as I was able to get to chat daily with other successful business owners who helped elevate my business intelligence. Then in 2017 at the GIE+EXPO (now the Equip Exposition) I was able to meet Naylor in "real life." Our friendship continues to strengthen over the years and I appreciate everything he does behind the scenes for the lawn care community. I dedicate this book to the Lawn Care Rookie and hope the content herein will help transform businesses in a similar way to how Naylor's content positively impacted my business endeavors. Thank you for your friendship and all you do for the community.

Contents

Preview

This is the third book of a trilogy. In my first book, *Cut That Grass and Make That Cash* I shared the journey of how I started a lawn care business out of the trunk of a 1997 Honda Accord and eventually through learning "in the school of hard knocks" built a successful business. Throughout that book, I emphasized the many mistakes I made and the valuable lessons learned through those experiences. Then, in the second book *Best Business Practices for Landscapers,* I highlighted the habits, traits, and commonalities I noticed from top landscapers in the Green Industry. As host of the Green Industry Podcast, I have had the unique opportunity to interview many of the top lawn and landscape, business leaders. Over time it became very evident to me that there were many shared similarities between those who are winning both in their businesses and in their personal lives. To complete the trilogy in this book it is my goal to deliver the fundamentals, the X's and O's, the tactics that will help you build a more efficient company and make more money!

1

Know Your Numbers

#1 - Know Your Numbers

The popular and fun topics to discuss when building a successful business are typically sales, marketing, and operations. We will dive deep into those topics throughout this book, but first and foremost, I want to address what I believe to be the most important element in building a better business. In operating a profitable business, knowing your numbers is of the utmost importance. The bottom line is that in order to boost your bottom line it is necessary to know your numbers. This trendy term is often mentioned amongst lawn and landscape industry leaders, but let's dive deeper into what it actually means to know our numbers.

#2 - Create a Budget Each Month

You have to be intentional to get your numbers right and tight. The dreaded "B" word can be scary. For some people when they hear the word budget they feel restricted. Many folks want freedom and feel like a budget limits their ability to have fun. The truth of the matter, however, is that those who set a specific budget and then track their expenses feel in control of their finances. When you know precisely what is going on with your money it brings about peace, calmness, and typically an abundance of information to guide wise decisions in the future. It is necessary to have a budget not only for our personal expenses but for our business as well.

Let's start with the personal budget. As a business consultant, I have been an advisor to many lawn care business owners. They come from all walks of life and various circumstances. One of the first things we examine in developing a master plan for their business is what salary they need to pay themself? This number should not be pulled out of thin air, but rather well calculated based on what it actually takes to run their household. Of course, that number will fluctuate based on many variables such as marital status, the number of children, living expenses, debt, retirement goals, etc. Each month is different but we research what the average month looks like and what are their annual household expenses?

Knowing your numbers is not just pivotal in your business, but also in your personal money decisions. This is a skill that we should have been taught in high school, but unfortunately, many of us were not taught the basic techniques of how to budget and track our spending. It used to surprise me when I would consult with a new client that they did not have a specific budget for each month. Many were just winging it or would tell me their wife takes care of all of that. A specific budget for your personal finances each month will help you feel organized and in control and that will ultimately help position you to be more poised, confident, and focused in leading your business.

Once things are in order at home, it's now also important that there is a separate budget for the business. For my business budget, I simply use Google Sheets. I check this document daily, monitoring that the game plan is being executed properly. Each month I create a new tab at the bottom of the spreadsheet so that each month has its own specific budget. In cell A1 I start with my fixed costs. I am able to copy and paste these in each month because they are the same amount each month and I have these on auto ACH or debit. To track that each expense was paid on time in column "F" I simply fill in the date once the expense is paid. In a normal month there are at least twenty fixed costs, here is an example of what the first couple of rows look like in my business budget.

Fixed Cost (A)	Payable To (B)	Amount (C)	Due Date (D)	Payment Type (E)	Date Paid (F)
Email	Google G Suite	$5.40	2nd	Auto Debit	11-2
Quickbooks	QB Online	$50	4th	Auto Debit	11-4

Then underneath the fixed costs section, I have a variable costs section. I take the time before the first of each month to create a unique budget for the upcoming month. In the example below you can see that I budgeted for the tag renewal and emissions for a work vehicle. This expense only happens once a year, but I planned for it ahead of the month of the expense.

Variable Cost	Payable To	Amount	Date Paid
Tag Renewal	Forsyth County	$20.60	11-9
Emissions	Derka	$25	11-10

Depending on the month, the variable cost rows can be extensive but it's important to be ready and prepared to pay all the bills on time. Being alert and aware of what it costs to operate the business helps keep me focused on being diligent to keep the cash flow flowing! It's an automatic part of my morning routine to check the business checking accounts each morning. As I do that I am also updating and tracking the business budget to make sure everything is happening according to the blueprint. By staying on top of this there are typically no "surprises."

And although I use my custom-made Google Sheets to track the business budget, for my personal budget I use the Dave Ramsey, Every Dollar app to track my personal expenses. I typically spend about fifteen minutes each morning syncing my personal expenses in the Every Dollar app, scanning through online business banking to make sure everything looks right, and also updating my business budget spreadsheet. I consider this daily maintenance. In addition to my daily effort to "know my numbers" I have a first-class team that helps add their expertise to ensure I know my number and the business has a healthy future.

#3 - Hire A Good Bookkeeper

One of the greatest regrets I have as a small business owner is that I waited too long until I hired a reputable bookkeeper. For years in my effort to save money, I was the company's bookkeeper. I would go through my receipts, syncing everything to QB Online, but the reality was this was not being a good steward of my time. This was the classic mistake of the owner working in the business when I could have been utilizing my time to work on the business. Eventually, I met an outstanding couple Megan and Joey Coberly, and hired them to take care of the books. They are professionals who keep my business organized while saving me TIME! In addition to basic bookkeeping, once a month we do a profit meeting where they analyze the monthly financial reports helping me discover what the business is telling me to focus on. The numbers tell a story and by having quality professional bookkeepers I am able to discern what exactly the story is. Then I can make the necessary adjustments to ensure the business is heading in the right direction. Having a quality professional bookkeeper is imperative to keeping your business's finances organized and above board. Keith Kalfas says, "you can't afford not to have a bookkeeper."

#4 - Hire a Good Accountant

When I was in high school I was considering a career as an accountant. During my senior year I actually worked at an accounting firm, good ole 415 Group in Canton, Ohio. I would go to class in the morning then spend the afternoons working as an assistant to the president of the accounting firm. Although that job provided generous pay for a senior in high school, I quickly realized I needed to find a new career path, because accounting was not for me! I realized staying up to date on current tax laws and penalties was not as interesting as staying up to date with the latest College Football BCS Rankings.

Just like a bookkeeper can save you time, so can a good accountant. A qualified professional accountant will help you structure your business appropriately, reduce tax liability, prevent hefty tax penalties and help you take advantage of tax deductions as well as keep you informed with the ever-changing tax laws. Having both a good bookkeeper and a good accountant on your team is critical.

#5 - Hire A Good Tax and Financial Planner

Do not worry, we will get to the fun topics soon discussing what power equipment to buy and all the enjoyable aspects of building a business. But, it's important that we establish how vital knowing our numbers is. In addition to having a reputable, professional bookkeeper and accountant, it's also crucial to have a good financial planner on the team. Some financial services offer an all-in-one service to cover your bookkeeping, accounting, and tax/financial planning needs. Many of those packages can be great and get the job done. I prefer to have multiple people on my team, just to have a "checks and balances" approach and make sure I have a multitude of counselors. Whether you go à la carte or select an all-in-one, having each a bookkeeper, accountant, and tax and financial planner is paramount.

A financial planner can help set you up for success with investing. This is an important part of the formula for knowing your numbers. As we mentioned at the beginning of the chapter, it's a big deal to get your numbers tight and right. As we sell jobs, we need to be accounting for not just the labor rate, job materials, overhead, but also the owner's salary and our future goals. Having an understanding of the full overall financial picture will give us clarity and confidence to bid our work at a rate that will set us up for lasting success.

6 - Stay Current on Quarterly Taxes

With the help of a good bookkeeper, accountant, and tax planner you should know with precision how much your tax bill is each quarter. This will help you to budget accurately to make sure the money is saved and available to pay these ever-important quarterly taxes on time. I understand that we may have readers in Australia, New Zealand, across Europe, Canada, and other areas. Your tax laws may differ quite a bit from ours here in the USA. But, the common denominator is we have to pay our taxes and plan accordingly so they are paid in full and on time. Here in America getting behind with federal or state taxes can be detrimental. The penalties and interest are high. This can cause stress, anxiety and be a big hindrance to success in business. Therefore, it is a serious matter to be intentional on the front end to make sure we set aside money ahead of time so we can pay our taxes on time.

Here in the United States the quarterly taxes typically follow this schedule:

Payment Period	Due Date
January 1 – March 31	April 15
April 1 – May 31	June 15
June 1 – August 31	September 15
September 1 – December 31	January 15 of the following year.

Again, trying to tackle all of this alone can be daunting. Get the right people on the bus by hiring a qualified, reputable, dependable, honest, professional bookkeeper, accountant, tax planner, and financial planner. This investment is a part of building a good foundation so that our businesses can have lasting success.

#7 - Get a Financial Accountability Partner

When an animal is isolated, often the prey will pick it off and have its next meal. However, when animals stay in packs, they have a level of protection with each other looking out for their neighbor. In business, it can be very beneficial to have a mentor who is willing to help keep an eye on your numbers and make sure you are headed in the right direction.

You may wonder, isn't a good bookkeeper, accountant, tax, and financial planner enough? Well, they certainly are a part of the winning formula. But, personally, I only meet with my bookkeepers once a month and accountant, tax planner, and financial planner once a quarter. It can also be very helpful to have another set of eyes scanning the number and making sure we are on point. The larger companies in the industry have

CFO's and others on their teams who are continuously analyzing the numbers. Even though we may start with smaller revenues it is a good habit to get into. Make sure there are multiple eyes analyzing the story your numbers are telling. In the multitude of counselors, there is safety.

2

Highly Effective Systems and Policies

In this chapter, we will look at some more practical tactics to dot your i's and cross your t's to help ensure you have a strong foundation for your business.

8 - Get Legal and Legit

The types of professionals outlined in the previous chapter should have adequate insights into how to structure your business. Since our readership is international, there are many variables and complexities to structuring your business. The main point is that you want to make sure you have the proper licenses, insurances and that you are set up both professionally and legally.

9 - Deposit 100% of Your Revenue Into Your Business Checking Account

Once you are properly signed up with the appropriate governing author-ities, it should be easy to open a business checking account at your local bank or credit union. Personally, I have found Mike Michalowicz's plan from his book *Profit First* to be very helpful in structuring my business banking. Whether you have multiple bank accounts as Michalowicz suggests or you have one business account, either way, it's necessary to make sure you are disciplined to deposit ALL business income into your business checking account. Even if "Sweet Sue" pays you cash or cuts the check to your name personally, be faithful to put 100% of business income into your business checking account.

Not only will this help you to legally abide by the laws of the land, but it also shows you the true numbers in your business. The goal is for the data we analyze to be 100% accurate. This will help you make better-informed decisions in building a successful business. Therefore, it's important to make sure all income is accounted for correctly. With the trend of many customers preferring to pay by card, this should be easier nowadays than it used to be. Nevertheless, it's worthy to reiterate that keeping the finances clean and true is to your benefit in the long run.

#10 - Don't Intermingle Your Personal Expenses With Your Business Account

Keeping your personal expenses separate from your business expenses is essential. Step one as we mentioned is to make sure that all business income goes into your business account. Then, step two is to stay disciplined to make sure business expenses are paid out of the business account and personal expenses are paid out of the personal account. Special guest Kory Ballard shared on the Green Industry Podcast that when he went to sell his lawn care business he realized how critical it was that business and personal are completely separate.

Although there can be some gray areas and we can "justify" our sloppiness, at the end of the day it's a good habit to get into making sure we never compromise and keep the business expenses and personal expenses separate. Your accountant and tax planner can help guide you into how to pay yourself from the business. After you get paid, then that money is available for all your personal expenses. But be sure to follow the systems and protocols to keep the business and personal independent of each other. This will help you keep the books clean and have authentic and true numbers to work with when analyzing the data to make informed decisions as you build the business.

#11 - Open up a Separate Savings Account For Quarterly Taxes

Out of the 101 proven ways to increase efficiency and make more money in lawn care described in this book, this practical strategy is by far one of the most important. Getting behind on taxes has led to the downfall of many businesses. For others who were able to weather the storm and pay off their big tax bills, it left scars and wounds with the uneasy memories of the stress and anxiety of owing Uncle Sam. While a good bookkeeper, accountant, and tax planner should guide you to proactively make sure you are paying your quarterly taxes in full and on time, it's worth reiterating in this chapter as well along with providing a clear path of how to do it.

Most business checking accounts come with the option of also having a savings account linked to the business checking account. This makes it convenient and easy to transfer money between business checking and savings. This is a good rhythm to get into to make sure that we are intentionally saving the necessary monies for our quarterly taxes. It's one thing to be aware of how much we owe and the due dates, etc. But, it's another thing to make sure we actually have the funds set aside to pay these tax bills.

The famous saying is, "Know *Your* Numbers". *Your* is italicized to emphasize your numbers will likely be different than the numbers for Chuck in the Truck and Rick's Mowing. There are so many variables to consider, but that's why I recommend hiring financial pros who will help you understand how much money you need to be setting aside to make sure you are able to pay your quarterly taxes on time. If you are in the United States, you can also get set up with the EFTPS and that system makes it super convenient and easy to pay your taxes online.

Typically, it's the hardest to save at first. But, once you get into the routine it often becomes easier and with the help of the financial pros on your team, you will start to identify the trends and have a clearer understanding of how much you should be saving.

#12 - Get The Proper Insurance

Recently I attended the Lawntrepreneur Academy Live training event in Novi, Michigan. While there a lawn bro named Kyle came up to me and showed me his hand. I instantly turned my head in shock. It was a scary sight to see the aftermath of what Kyle's hand looked like after it had been severely damaged after a recent injury. Kyle went on to explain to me that because of the injury he was unable to work and because he was the main laborer in his business, eventually, he lost all his customers. Long story short, he lost all his revenue. This put Kyle into a tailspin where he battled depression and was scrambling to figure out his future. Thankfully, Kyle found the content from Keith Kalfas, Brian Fullerton, and others in the industry and was able to rekindle hope as he strategizes his comeback.

Kyle asked me if he could share his story on the Green Industry Podcast because he did not have insurance and wanted to warn as many who would listen to get properly insured asap. Depending on the size and structure of your business, the insurance plan that is best for you may vary. Do your research to compare and contrast the pros and cons of the various insurances. Best practices are to have at a minimum: general liability, workers comp, commercial auto insurance, and commercial property insurance. There are other insurances to consider but this is a starting point. There may be some initial sticker shock with your insurance rates, but that's why we say we know your numbers. When your business is licensed, insured, and legit, the overhead builds up fast. That's why we need to take the initiative to truly understand what it costs to operate our business so that we can price our services accordingly.

#13 - Save for Winter

Don't worry, we will get into the fun topics such as getting and keeping customers soon. But, having an honest overview of what it actually costs to professionally run the business is fundamental in order to better understand why we must price our services accurately.

One of my favorite lawn care YouTubers is Johnny Mow. Johnny is one of the first guys I started watching on YouTube back in the day and he by far provides some of the best value on his video channels. Johnny currently is "solo and proud" as he has recently downsized his business after the stress of running multiple crews. Johnny found a sweet spot in his work/life balance where he now has the margin to spend quality time with his wife and daughters.

A key to Johnny's success is his financial discipline to save his winter fund by labor day. Johnny is proactive to crunch his numbers and knows what it takes to operate his household expenses during those brutal Pennsylvania winters. He then makes his target goal to save that amount by labor day each year. This helps put a pep in his step throughout the spring rush to make hay while the sun's out. Johnny, then diligently saves a good portion of his money into that winter fund as he year after year successfully reaches his goal by labor day.

One of the most frequently asked questions we receive at the Green Industry Podcast is how to produce revenue in the off-season and winter? When the grass and bushes are not growing how do you make money? While there are multiple unique opportunities to produce revenue in the winter months, the tried and true plan is to simply save enough cash to carry you through winter like Johnny Mow.

#14 - Have Clear Billing Policies

Perhaps this has been a lot to digest thus far. At face value operating a lawn, business seems easy. Just cut that grass and make that cash right? Beyond the blades of grass that are cut, the yards of mulch that are spread, and maybe even the pallets of sod that are laid, there are the people. Our customers are real people and they have lives just like we do. They likely have full schedules and their phones, like ours, are probably pinging with the latest notification. The last thing on their mind is making sure we are paid on time, in full, and that our business is operating profitably.

We came out of the gate in this book thus far emphasizing some practical tactics that involve us spending money. It costs money to hire financial services, get properly insured, pay our taxes on time, and that barely even scratches the surface of the overhead it costs to operate a successful lawn and landscape business.

Therefore, it is important that we have cash flow. We will discuss developing our prices later in the book, but I want to mention at the onset the ever-important topic of billing. Many businesses are on life support or even fail because of poor cash flow. Robbing Peter to pay Paul is no way to operate a business. In addition to operating efficiently and at the right price, it is also significant that you have a clear billing procedure and stick to it.

Each month AT&T takes $69.99 out of my bank account for my internet bill. I pay and they provide internet services. Guess what, if I don't pay, no internet. It's the same with my electric bill. If I don't pay, no lights. And the list goes on and on. As I showed you a glimpse of my overhead costs on the spreadsheet in chapter one, most of these everyday expenses are set up on auto-pay. It's the way business is done. It's convenient for the customer and brings in steady reliable cash flow to the service provider. Easy peasy.

However, in the lawn care industry, many businesses operate with a clunky, confusing billing process. Could you imagine if I called AT&T and told them I would put their payment in a ziplock bag in my grill? LOL! I don't think they would accept that. What about if I at least put it under the mat on the front door? Nope, they have their billing policies. They clearly communicated to me when I ordered their service how I had to set up auto-pay. What if I told Verizon Wireless I would pay them in cash for my cell phone bill? Just come knock on my door when I get home from work and I will square up with them. Nope, they have their billing policy as well. And I have conveniently set up auto-pay. And if I don't pay, Verizon will cut my phone off and ding my credit score.

These large companies are very clear about what their billing policies are. Leaving checks under mats, in grills, or handing off cash at your back door is not part of their policies. However, this is how many lawn businesses still conduct business.

Paver Pete was recently a special guest on the Green Industry Podcast. I asked Pete about how he suggests collecting payment for work. He explained the importance of building trust with the customer and also briefly explained how some states have certain laws about how much you can collect throughout the project. Then, to my surprise, he shared that if it's a $4,000 job, he would just collect a $4,000 payment for the job upfront. Now, I had heard of a 50% deposit, 50% upon completion. Personally, I started doing that until transitioning to the ⅓ deposit plan. ⅓ when starting the project then ⅓ upon completion. But, Pete blew me away with his confidence that if you build trust then you simply ask the customer to pay 100% of the bill upfront. Even though you may not come and complete the work for a few weeks. He went on to explain that for jobs north of $100,000 you may want to consider a payment draw schedule. But on small jobs under $10,000 just ask for the full amount if legal in your state.

It's shocking to me how many lawn maintenance companies will come and mow all month, then leave the bill at the end of the month. Meanwhile, all months that business is stuck paying out its overhead and labor and still has not received payment for the work performed. Then, with the clunky collection systems, more time will pass until receiving the money. This is problematic and can cause great damage to the health of a business.

The solution is to get paid before you do the work. Here in the Atlanta market, it is common to do pre-pay. Customers are willing to pay on the 1st of each month (in advance) for that month's services. Let's say you charge a customer $300 per month to mow, edge, trim and blow. You service their property from March 1 - November 1. With business management software such as Jobber, you can simply charge the customer's card on file on the agreed-upon date.

Step 1, when quoting the work, be very clear with the customer that payment is due on the 1st of each month prior to the work being done, that is your policy. Then step two once they agree to your rate and service offerings, collect the customer's card on file. Step three then is to simply charge the customer's card on file on the agreed-upon date. This makes it convenient for the customer and helps boost your cash flow. Now, you should have the money ahead of time to be able to tackle the month's expenses. The more confident you get in your billing policies the easier it is to communicate your policy to your customer and the more successful you will be at getting paid in full and on time. That is my recommended payment plan.

For those of you rolling your eyes saying that's impossible in my market. Then, at the very least, collect the payment on the day you provide the service if you are going to charge per maintenance. I have a coaching client who lives in rural Illinois. He has a customer that needs their "weeds" cut bi-weekly. And so immediately after he gets done with their service he sits in his truck, pulls out his business management software app, and charges the customer card on file. If that is the route you want to take then at least be very clear with the customer that upon completion of each service their card on file will be charged. (Visit GreenIndustryPodcast.com if you are interested in one-on-one coaching).

#15 - Raise Your Rate Regularly

Jaymz Shields recently made his debut as a special guest on the Green Industry Podcast. Jaymz owns and operates 2nd Mile Servants Lawncare in Tennessee. Before going full-time in lawn care Jamyz worked at Chick-fil-a. He shared on the show that one thing he noticed while working at Chick-fil-a is that they frequently, incrementally raised the prices on their food. Those delicious spicy chicken sandwiches would consistently cost more and more. However, it would happen so subtly that you rarely notice.

A phenomenal habit to get into operating a successful lawn care business is to get used to consistently raising your rates. Depending on the year inflation may rise 3-5% or more. Even if the numbers are right and tight from the beginning, just staying ahead of inflation dictates us to annually raise our rates. The best practice is to notify your current clients each year before the season begins of their slight rate adjustment. At greenindustrypodcast.com we have our ever-popular rate increase letter template for sale that professionally and concisely communicates with customers why and how much their rate is going up for the new season. It's recommended to email this out a few weeks before the start of the season. Then of course for new customers, whose work we have not yet bid yet, make sure to calculate the new rate as you bid the job.

It's surprising to me how many businesses maintain the same rates year after year. Meanwhile, inflation and other expenses are on the rise. Therefore, it's required to make it a part of the rhythm of operating our business. Just as Chick-fil-a incrementally and frequently raises the price of their waffle fries, we must raise our rates.

#16 - Track Your Time

As we start off this book with the ultra-important emphasis on knowing your numbers, it's important to mention that those numbers are not just financially related. Tracking our time is a crucial component to increasing efficiency and earning more money as well. The Lawn Care Millionaire on YouTube highlights, in video after video, we in the lawn care business are in the business of selling time.

In future chapters, we will explore how we can fine-tune the business to operate at maximum efficiency. Getting the work done in a quality manner at lightning-fast speed is critical but also is being able to measure how long a property will take us and then bidding that work accordingly.

Having a time log and keeping an accurate record of what time we start work on a property, what time we finished the work, and how many employees were on the job is a good place to begin. With these data points, you can calculate how many man-hours were spent on the job and what you earned per man-hour on the job based on the current rate you are charging the customer so you can determine if the rate needs to be adjusted. The Pricing Matrix spreadsheet is a product that I actually developed with my friend Dr. Frank Holleman that makes it easy to plug in your data and then have the algorithm instantly spit out the information you need to clearly identify what you are earning per man hour per property.

Tracking your time on each job and property not only helps analyze your performance but also provides data for quoting future jobs. It was once said that time is the wisest counselor of all. If we take the initiative to track our time then we can have the data available to help guide us to take our business to the next level.

3

Strategically Selecting Your Service Offerings and Target Customer

#17 - Clearly Establish What Services You Offer

The average property has several possible services they may need. Recognizing how we can solve our customers' problems is important. There are multiple approaches to building a profitable business and in this chapter, I want to survey why it's important to develop a plan of what services you want your business to provide. Some companies prefer to be a one-stop-shop that services any and every possible lawn and landscape needs. While others will offer a few services and sub-contract out the other services. While, others find a niche they specialize in, stay in their lane and only offer that service and share referrals for the other services. Each of these paths has pros and cons. Once you determine what areas you want your business to focus on, then you will know where to invest your time, energy, and resources to gain the proper knowledge and equipment to become an expert and build a profitable business. Clarity on what services you offer will also aid in executing excellent marketing strategies. Here is a shortlist of services that many properties may request:

- Lawn mowing
- Mulch, pine straw
- Seasonal flowers
- Irrigation
- Lighting
- Tree services
- Plant Installation
- Fertilizer and weed control programs
- Mosquito control

When I started my lawn care business in 2011, I was broke, busted, and disgusted and was just trying to earn every dollar I could to just stay afloat. I foolishly said yes to any opportunity to bring in revenue. My zeal and passion were untamed. When a customer asked me, "Can you do this, can you do that?" my answer, nearly 100% of the time, was "Yes!" I thought being Johnny on the Spot and proactively agreeing to solve my customers' problems was smart. It was bringing in revenue, but what I failed to calculate was that doing anything and everything was not a profitable use of my time. I was gaining no traction because I was continuously putting out a new fire. Instead of gaining momentum, I was quickly becoming oppressed and attempting to outearn my stupidity. I lacked the proper knowledge, equipment, and staffing to profitably run a business that offered seemingly unlimited services. I quickly found myself not only mowing grass but also installing sod, mulch, flowers, pine straw, etc.. additionally, I was also cleaning gutters, applying fertilizer, helping people move furniture, pressure washing and the list goes on and on. Recently on an episode of the Green Industry Podcast, I joked about these rookie mistakes with Jason Creel and he mentioned to me that he started out making those same mistakes and he even added to the list when he shared that he had a customer ask him to come inside the house and help them hang a picture. As rookies, it's tempting to meet every need, but there needs to be a designed plan to only offer the services that your skills, systems, and operation are fine-tuned to complete.

I agreed to these jobs because I saw them as money flowing into my bank account. However, what I did not forecast is that my lack of experience would cause even more money to leave my bank account from my mistakes and I quickly became a rat in the wheel. I broke a window pressure washing, broke another window gutter cleaning, and burnt a customer's lawn over-applying fertilizer that had a high amount of nitrogen in it. What I did not add into the equation was replacing windows, re-sodding yards, etc… My eagerness to say yes and earn money cost me money in the long run because my business did not have the proper equipment, systems, employees, and sub-contractors to handle such a wide variety of service offerings.

I hope you will learn from my early mistakes. I experienced the classic example of the inmates running the asylum. My customers were essentially running my business. I was the "yes" man doing whatever they needed. Thankfully, I was able to pivot out of that negative pattern and take control of the business. Eventually, I developed a clear blueprint and stood firm to my boundaries. My recommendation is in your business to select what services you desire to offer and build your business around that. For the services you don't offer, find a trusted company you can refer the work to. This will help you add value to your customers and help avoid the traps of trying to do it all yourself.

#18 - Identify Your Target Customer

Throughout the next few chapters, we will explore the ever-important topic of marketing. Piggybacking off the previous chapter, it's important that we have clear boundaries on what services we offer, what services we don't offer, and what services we refer to another trusted company. The next step is now to identify who is our target customer? Answering this question will then help us to formulate a strategic marketing plan.

The age-old debate in the lawn care and landscape industry is what is a better business plan, servicing residential or commercial properties? The honest answer is it depends. Some companies go all-in on commercial work, while others solely focus on residential customers in a route dense area, while others offer a hybrid of both commercial and residential work.

The pros of residential work are that in most regions there are lots of neighborhoods that you can target with your marketing and establish great route density. By providing quality work and keeping the pipeline full with a solid marketing plan, it can be very convenient to establish your service area in a local community. The route density helps with efficiency and it's rewarding to be the "go-to" business in a local neighborhood or community. The cons of residential are it's a typically higher volume which means more vetting customers and dealing with more potential PITA (pain in the a**) customers.

The pros of commercial work are often that it's convenient to serve larger projects. Less windshield time and more time on the property getting paid for your labor. The cons however are often the bidding wars for commercial work can be cutthroat and payment can usually be on net 30,60,90 or even 120-day terms.

Personally, after dabbling for years in commercial work I eventually threw in the towel. Losing work because someone else had a lower bid "stung". I'm a loyal and faithful person and so if I'm doing a good job, I appreciate customers who continue the relationship. When someone wants to move "in another direction" because of price, it just doesn't sit well with me. With residential work, I noticed very minimal attrition. And when there was attrition it was typically because a customer moved. Although I have had some sour experiences with commercial work, I have many friends who love it. They make good money doing it and have built their businesses around acquiring commercial properties.

In conclusion, before really developing your specific marketing plan, sit down and really think and analyze carefully what services you want to offer and to whom? There is not necessarily a right and wrong answer. Many combinations have proven to be successful. But, what is needed is that you determine what route you want to take so that you can develop a good marketing strategy and have clear boundaries with your customers and potential customers.

#19 - Identify Your Service Area

Once you clearly determine the services you offer and who your target customer is, it is important now to select what area you plan to provide service to. This information is helpful in developing your marketing plan and it's significant to know so you can better vet customers. The old-fashioned yet effective way to do this is to put a map on the wall in your office. Then draw a circle or whatever shape necessary around the area you select to work in.

There are many variables to consider when selecting how wide of an area you want to offer service to. Typically, the tighter you can get your service area the better. This will help to really fine-tune your marketing plan and get the work done efficiently. Here in Atlanta, because the traffic is so terrible, route density is pivotal. Perhaps if your business is in more of a rural area it might make sense to have a larger service area. And in some circumstances where folks are installing large ticket price installations, it may make sense to travel a little further for high-paying jobs. But, if you are planning to execute basic lawn maintenance, route density is recommended.

4

A Successful Marketing Strategy

#20 - Know Your Market

Love him or hate him, Bill Belichick is one of the winningest coaches in NFL history. Even though I am a Cleveland Browns fan, for whatever reason, I am always fascinated to catch a Bill Belichick press conference. It's intriguing to hear Belicheck's perspective on his upcoming opponent. Sometimes it seems like he knows the opposing team better than they do. There is a lot that business leaders can take away from the expertise of this successful football coach. It's important that we understand our market. Studying both our competition and customers has its benefits. Just like a good football coaching staff will study the details to find any slight edge they have. As business leaders, if we want to separate ourselves from the pack we must take the time to have a comprehensive understanding of our market and follow our path to victory.

We will dive further into this process in the chapter about networking. But a brief overview is that by asking questions of the right people we can gather the information necessary to understand our market. I like to start with the nursery and supplier yards. By cultivating good relationships with the leadership of these providers I'm able to ask them questions about my competitors' prices as tap into their understanding of the landscape market in my area. They have a lot of information and if you connect with the right folks they will happily help you understand what areas spend the most money on landscaping and what the average rates are in the industry.

#21 - Letter or Wrap Your Vehicle

Research studies conclude various results in regards to how many touches it requires to make a sale. The common denominator though is that the more quality touches or impressions prospective customers experience the better your chance to gain a new client. If your crew is working in a route dense area then having your vehicles and trailers lettered or wrapped can be a huge marketing success. When your vehicle and equipment set up is parked in front of a customer's property while your team is executing the service it becomes a giant billboard. As folks drive by they have the opportunity to see your company being represented.

The space on your vehicle and or trailer is a place to communicate to prospects who your company is and what services you provide. The rule of thumb with marketing with your vehicle and trailers is that less is more. Showcasing a clean presentation of your company's name, logo, phone number and website is more than enough. Anything beyond that and it starts to get cluttered and the message you are sending to the customer may be negative. The goal is to make sure the truck and trailer are clean and has a clear presentation and representation of who you are.

#22 - Utilize a Detailed Professional Voicemail

Your business phone voicemail is a great opportunity to both vet customers and market your services. Now, the best practice is to have a team member answer the phone when a customer or potential customer calls. But, for those occasions, if someone calls after office hours or perhaps you are on the other line and it goes to voicemail you want to make the most of that opportunity.

A couple of tips I learned in broadcasting school that may help you create the best voicemail possible. Stand up when you record the voicemail recording. This will help create some authority and confidence in your voice. Second, smile as you leave the voicemail recording. Third, feel free to record as many takes as you want. Depending on what kind of phone you have, it should be simple to re-record the voicemail until you are satisfied with how it sounds and represents your business. In regards to the script and what information to include on the voicemail. I would recommend stating the name of your business, clearly communicating what your service area is and what services you provide, and then a brief message that you will return their call soon and request they leave their name and number.

Sample: Hello you have reached Clean Cut Lawn Care. We provide lawn maintenance services in Duluth and Suwanee, Georgia. Please leave your name, number, and reason for your call and one of our team members will contact you soon. Thank you and have a nice day!

That voice mail is a tool for marketing as it explains who you are and what services you provide and where. It also is a great way to get customers and save time. If a potential customer listens to your voicemail but realizes they live outside your service area or perhaps are looking for a different type of service they may hang up. Saving you time. Several people in our industry use Mr. Producer to record professional-grade voice mail greetings. You can DM him @MrProducerUSA on Instagram.

#23 - Create Professional Business Cards

Recently I overheard someone boasting that they haven't had business cards in years. They shared that they could be reached on LinkedIn or Instagram. While social media is an incredible way to communicate with clients and potential clients, a good old-fashioned business card still is effective. I recommend keeping them on hand in the truck and even in your team members' pockets throughout the workday. You never know when a neighbor or potential customer may stop and ask for a card or more information about your company. If you can swiftly hand them a professional business card. The card should answer their questions about what services you provide and how they contact you.

I don't want to beat a dead horse as I previously mentioned the importance of clean, neat, and to the point with the truck and trailer messaging as well as the voice mail, but to emphasize the same point, keep the business card simple and straightforward.

#24 - Wear Clean Professional Uniforms

As someone who has already spent a decade in the field, I totally understand that comfort is very important to those performing lawn and landscape services. We can't be out there working in the elements in a three-piece suit. There needs to be a level of comfort to what we wear that's in sync with the climate. Whether it's a hot summer day or a frigid cold bitter winter day make sure your team has the proper clothing. It is a best practice that employees' uniforms are clean and represent our company. You can get your company's logo put on t-shirts, golf shirts, hoodies, jackets, hats, etc... It's important that staff are in uniform while working. For starters, it's a way to market and it also builds trust with your customers and morale with your team members.

#25 - Maximize Word of Mouth Referrals

It does take relational intelligence and experience to know when you hand someone a card if at this moment you are building trust that could lead to a future sale or if it's time to close the deal. Typically, when you receive correspondence from a potential customer and they are a "word of mouth" referral from a pleasant customer, it's GO TIME! These are often rare but usually golden opportunities. The person reaching out to you as a "word of mouth" referral probably trusts the person who referred your business to this potential new customer. So the level of trust is already established to an extent. These hot leads commonly result in work so in the famous words of Caleb Auman, "Don't screw it up!" Or said in a brighter positive way, do your best to convert this lead into a sale if there is proper alignment between the referral and your services. This is one of those rare times when being "Johnny on the Spot" is generally worth it.

#26 - Capitalize on Google My Business

At the time of writing this book, Google is the world's largest search engine. Getting your business listed on Google My Business is very easy and well worth it. This is a way to possibly convert those who are searching for your service on Google search or maps into customers, for free! You can collect Google reviews and post fresh content and pictures on your profile to showcase your business to the world. To get started, just "Google" Google My Business, and the instructions will guide you through the simple process to get your business profile created and verified.

#27 - Website

A good website can really help communicate your company's story with its visitors. An effective website can establish trust and convert visitors into customers. Best practices are for a lawn care website to be clean and simple while being easy to navigate.

Your website is an excellent opportunity to share a gallery of photos of your work. It's good to include real pictures and videos of work your company does, not generic stock footage! Be authentic and communicate to website visitors the quality of your company with actual original pictures. Even though using real photos is recommended, make sure these are quality pictures.

Your website is also a place to showcase your reviews. Your customer's testimonials build credibility and can be very influential to visitors that your company may be the solution to the website visitors problem.

The ultimate goal of the website is to get visitors to either call you or to fill out a form so you can receive their contact info and get in touch with them. A common practice is to offer a "Free Quote" form. This form must include a space where you gather the visitor's email address and phone number so you can get in contact with them.

#28 - Collect Online Reviews from Happy Customers

Once your business is successfully on Google My Business, it builds your social proof and credibility by requesting that your customers leave you a rating and review. The more convenient you make this for your customers, the more likely they are to leave a review. Emailing or texting them the link when they are at a point of being very pleased with your work is what I have found to work best. For example, if you just completed a sod installation and the customer is ecstatic and expressing their gratitude towards you. Capitalize on that momentum and ask them if they could share their excitement on a Google Review. Then, share the link with them. And after they leave the review make sure to thank them for taking the time to do so.

After being ripped off a couple of times in my life as a consumer, I am an avid reader of businesses' online reviews. I look at the quantity of how many reviews a business has and the quality of what people are saying about the business. It's in your best interest to build up your Google reviews with real, honest reviews as fast as possible.

#29 - Post Many Quality Pictures to Your Online Profiles

One of the beneficial features of Google My Business is that it lets you post pictures. With the remarkable technology of some of the cameras on smartphones today, a simple picture with the proper lighting with your smartphone can go a long way in communicating to potential customers about the quality of your work. The best practice is to showcase the best pictures of your work on Google My Business as well as on your website, business Facebook and Instagram pages. Whether it's a "before and after" picture or just a picture of the quality of your work, these pictures help build credibility and give you the opportunity to communicate to potential customers that you do outstanding work.

#30 - Master Email Marketing

How many times have you checked your email today? For me personally, I was pondering that question as well. I would venture to say that I checked my email on my smartphone twenty times today. It's almost become a habit that I don't even realize I'm doing. More than likely your customers and potential customers are checking their email multiple times a day as well.

In a future chapter, we will dive deeper into how your business is beyond just a service-based business. You actually also have a data collection business. If you consider selling your business one day the data you have collected or not collected can impact the price someone is willing to pay for your business if you decide to sell.

In the meantime, while you are operating your business, collecting emails and having strategic email marketing campaigns can have a massive ROI if done correctly and tactfully. Collecting your customers' email takes some intentionality but it's simple once you get into the swing of things. The easiest way to collect emails is through your website. When a potential customer fills out the "request a quote" form on your website, make sure to include a space where it's required they share their email. Secondly, when you have a customer call about your services simply ask them for their email over the phone.

Having a strong and growing email list will help you not only get new customers but also retain current customers. The more acquainted you get with the email marketing platform you use, you discover you can categorize your customers into different groupings and plan different emails for different groups. For example, you may want to have an email list for all your current customers and send them occasional emails adding value and just maintaining good clear communication about what to expect from your business. Never send out "spam" or attempt to over-sell. That will get you a fast unsubscribe, However, with the right ratios and a consistent dose of value your current customer may appreciate hearing from you and being in the loop of the things to consider during the different seasons of the year and how it affects their landscaping. Then at the right time do not be shy to upsell new services if it's in the customer's best interest. Here are a few examples and opportunities to consider.

#31 - Postcards Are Effective

Blitzing your service area with postcards or flyers can be a very effective way to get the word out about your business and the services you offer. When designing your postcard or flyer it may be very well worth it to hire a graphic designer to create a postcard or flyer that is aesthetically pleasing to look at while clearly communicating the messaging of your business. Since these will likely be produced in mass, making sure they look professional is worth the investment.

Distributing your postcards of flyers has a lot of variables. One of my favorite neighborhoods in Atlanta actually has a "birdie box" underneath the USPS mailbox for each resident in this neighborhood. With a convenient sidewalk that winds throughout the neighborhood, I found it best just to simply walk and place the business postcards in the birdie box. And note this was legal in that neighborhood, it was not the main mailbox. Here in the United States, it's illegal to put anything other than mail in the mailbox. The only folks permitted to open the mailbox are the mailbox owners and the postal employees. Therefore, you need to really understand the laws and protocols in the areas you want to distribute your flyers and postcards.

Another route to take is EDDM - Every Door Direct Mail. The United States Postal Service's EDDM program allows you to have your postcards delivered to individual neighborhoods, using carrier routes. This can be highly effective if you select the right area, send out your materials at the right time. I would recommend going with a larger postcard like a 6 x 11 and sending it out prior to peak season. In addition to marketing your regular services, you can also supplement the email marketing campaign with regular mail by sending out postcards promoting enhancement services such as core aerations, seasonal flowers, and other enhancement offerings.

#32 - Make the Most of Core Aeration Season

Core aerations are to be done at different times of the year depending on where you live and if you have cool or warm-season turf. Universally this service offers many benefits and should at least be considered in your lineup of offerings to a customer. Some of the benefits of core aerations are it relieves soil compaction, helps with thatch management, helps the grass develop deeper stronger roots, and provides a way for water and nutrients to enter the soil.

Prior to the core aeration season in your area, it is a solid idea to do an email marketing campaign. Let everybody on your list know the many of the benefits of core aeration when you plan to offer the service, and how they can sign up to get on your schedule for you to core aerate their lawn.

#33 - Consider Upselling Seasonal Flowers

Here in the Atlanta, Georgia area, it's best practice to install seasonal flowers twice a year, in the spring and fall. In the spring Georgia gets a beautiful makeover when people plant their gorgeous begonias and other spring flowers. In the fall many go with violas, pansies, Dusty Millers, and other flowers that can thrive in our mild winter temperatures. Whether you execute an email marketing campaign or do EDDM or both there is an opportunity for a massive ROI in upselling seasonal flowers. This adds instant curb appeal to properties and can be a nice revenue boost a couple of times a year.

Now as a disclaimer, your flower inventory and planting schedules will greatly vary depending on what region of the world you are in. But, the strategy of offering this service and properly marketing it to your customers can be profitable. The best place to start is at your local nursery. If you need further education about flowers, chat with the team there and let them show you the ropes.

#34 - Beware of the Deer!

Here in my market, we experience an interesting predicament during the winter months and that is that the deer are hungry! As much of deer's food supply shifts in the cooler months, the deer's appetite for pansies increases. Long story short, the deer will come into neighborhoods and eat the pansies.

The solution is deer netting! You can pick up the netting at a big box store and some metal landscape staples. Simply and neatly cover the pansies with the netting and that should thwart the deer's plans to eat the beautiful pansies you plant.

Now, we only have to use the deer netting for our winter seasonal flowers. By the springtime when we install begonias and other springtime flowers the deer usually do not disturb those since their regular food supply has returned when spring returns. If you live in a market where the deer might eat your flowers and you need to use deer netting, be sure to count the cost and accurately price out your flower work to include the deer netting. It does take quite a bit of time to make sure the net is thoroughly installed so the deer can't get through while still making the overall flower presentation look nice.

#35 - Upsell Other Enhancements

Many of the larger lawn and landscape businesses have thinner profit margins on their lawn maintenance divisions but have larger profit margins in their enhancement divisions. Whether it's sod, ground cover like mulch or pine straw, flowers, plants, or perhaps hardscape projects, these design and installation jobs can bring in big money. Once you identify what enhancements you want to offer your customers it's good to also strategize how and when you will market those enhancements.

Ground cover is a good place to start. Most customers want their garden beds to look fresh. Love it or hate it, pine straw is king here in many parts of the South. I grew up in Ohio where mulch was the predominant ground cover for garden beds. And personally, I love fresh mulch. I like the way it looks and even, oddly enough, the way it smells. But, here in Georgia folks love their pine straw.

Whether your region favors mulch or pine straw, it's good to establish a marketing plan to make sure you sell these services to your customers at a profitable rate. Both email marketing and EDDM plans can be a great way to communicate to your customers or potential customers that you offer this service. Before the opportune time to freshen up the garden beds consider running a targeted marketing campaign promoting these services.

5

Excellent Customer Service

Marketing is a huge component in acquiring new customers. Equally as important as getting new customers is keeping our customers! Retention is critical for lasting business success and in this chapter we will explore some things to consider to keep our customers happy and motivated to continue to purchase our services.

#36 - Treat People The Way You Want To Be Treated

Imagine if you hired a company to come and do some work at your home? What would you expect? How would you want to be treated? Personally, I would desire that the service professionals were skillful, qualified, polite, respectful (to my family and property) and that their price was fair and reasonable. I would also expect that they will communicate clearly. As business leaders, it's important that we attempt to put ourselves in our customers' shoes. The more we understand what they are thinking, feeling, and how they want to be treated, the more likely it is we can serve them well and retain loyal happy customers.

#37 - Business Management Software

The way technology and software are advancing is truly remarkable. Thankfully, for lawn and landscape business leaders there are plenty of options. Quality business management software makes it easy to enhance your customer service, close deals faster, and overall provide a professional touch with your communication with customers.

I remember when I started in 2011, I would print out paper invoice templates and fill them out with a pen while sitting in my truck at the customer's property. Then, I would either knock on the door and hand it to the customer in expectation of collecting payment or even leave it somewhere on their property. This old-fashioned clunky invoicing and billing system was not only inconvenient for my customer but also affected my cash flow.

When I began using Jobber in 2019, my customer service radically changed. Utilizing business management software helped me get paid faster and built my credibility with customers as all the quotes and invoices looked professional. No more paper template invoices with coffee stains on them. I would email my customers quotes through Jobber and land more sales. Then, when it came time to get paid, customers paid so much more swiftly when all they had to do was click a couple of buttons. Even better, as I began to get my recurring customers cards on file, cash flow really improved! No more checks in the mail!

Convenience is king. Customers appreciate it when we make things simple and easy for them. Although there is a learning curve to understand how to onboard your customers to a business management software solution, it's totally worth it. Using business management software to manage scheduling, quotes, jobs, invoicing, and more can be a huge win for your company and your customer. Use technology and software when necessary to make your customers' experience as simplified as possible.

#38 - Have Reputable Referrals to Offer Your Customers For Services You Don't Offer

It is very common that your customer will ask you if you provide a variety of services. If you answer no to a specific service, they will likely ask you if you know somebody who does. It can be a solution for your customer and to your benefit if you are ready and prepared for those questions with a trusted directory of professionals to who you can refer. Then, when your customer has a pleasant experience with the service professional you referred to, it will come back to boost that customer's trust in you. On the flip side, if you refer to somebody and they do a mediocre or poor job, then that can negatively affect your reputation. Be discerning and careful who you recommend someone, but it does help to be prepared because your customers will ask.

After I refer somebody to my customer then I usually give a heads up to my friend that I referred them to the customer. For example, there is a painter who does phenomenal work. He is very detail-oriented and reliable. One day my customer asked me if I was interested in painting the interior of his house. I laughed and said no thanks, but I instantly referred to my friend, the painter who does quality work. Immediately after the conversation with my customer, I called the painter and gave him a heads up that my client will likely be contacting him about a paint job. Lo and behold, my customer contacted the painter and the painter was "Johnny on the Spot" and came to their home and quoted the job. He ended up doing the work. It was a win, win, win, My customer was happy that his beautiful home got painted with excellence and he also was happy with me for referring him to my rock star painter! My painter friend was happy because he made bank on the job. And I was happy to see my friend get work and to know that my customers trust and appreciate me.

This is a process that takes time to figure out who in other trades does good work and is reliable. As you are assembling that directory of good pros, it may be wise if your customer asks for a referral and you don't know someone who will do a great job to simply tell them you don't know. But, as soon as you find those folks whether they are painters, roofers, electricians, plumbers, general handymen, irrigation specialists, etc make sure you refer them to your customers as your customers will appreciate you helping to solve their problem. And more than likely, those to whom you refer work will return the favor and send work your way.

#39 - Beware of the PITA's

As we discuss customer service I do want to at least mention that sometimes not all our customers should remain our clients. Throughout the vetting process, we need our discernment sharp to detect and avoid those potentially difficult customers. Occasionally, however, someone who is a pain in the *** may slip through the cracks and become a customer. Without a psychology briefing on why some humans invest so much effort in trying to be difficult, the bottom line is there are some customers that can actually be toxic and destructive to our business. When your PITA radar goes off, run!

There have been a few customers I have let go over the years. Typically, my first plan of attack is to substantially raise their rates. When I email them the rate increase letter they may reply that they are going to look for another service provider. And just like that, the issues may be resolved. However, I have done that before and the problematic customer agreed to the new rate. Although this is rare, it may come to the point of a well-written thoughtful email communicating that it's best to part ways. This can be hard but it's important that our businesses do not have any toxicity or poison from PITA clients. Over the years I've had to dismiss customers, sub-contractors, suppliers, and team members. This is necessary though and a part of the business to make sure we have the right people on the bus. Do your best to vet with good judgment but if you make a mistake, correct it before it's too late.

#40 - Have a Clear Contract

You need to protect your business for both the large and small landscape/hardscape jobs. Covering every contingency you can think of is important. This creates clarity for your customer and protects your butt legally.

#41 - Talk to the Husband and the Wife When Quoting Larger Jobs

One trend hopefully you are picking up on throughout this book is the importance of valuing both your time and your potential customers' time. When quoting larger landscape/hardscape jobs, schedule a meeting that includes both spouses. They will likely talk things over amongst themselves about the project before deciding if they are going to hire you or not. Therefore, it will be best for all parties involved if you schedule a meeting where you go over the scope of the project and pricing with both the husband and the wife. In the long run, this will save them and you a lot of time and keep things more simple.

#42 - Reread Texts and Emails Before Sending Them

Have you ever sent an email that was supposed to include an attachment but forgot to include the attachment? Have you ever sent or received a text where there was a typo? In our fast-paced culture, it can be easy to want to quickly reply to a customer's text or email. However, to ensure that each form of communication is accurate and professional, it's a fantastic habit to proofread texts and emails before sending them. This is a new habit that I actually developed within the last year. I will literally read out loud emails at least once before I send them to customers or potential customers. Surprisingly, as I listened to myself read the email or text I noticed something that could be changed or enhanced. Whether a word was wrongly autocorrected or structurally things could be said better, I will make the revision. Then reread it aloud again before sending it out. One way we can build and keep trust and credibility with our customers is by making sure our texts and emails are professional and to the point.

#43 - Be Mindful of When You Communicate With Customers

Respecting our customers' property, time and lives is so important. We are here to serve them and although we may eat, sleep and breathe our business 24-7, it's meaningful to be considerate of our customers' schedules. It's best to keep communication with texts and calls between 9:00 am - 6:00 pm unless the customer initiates the communication. For example, if a customer calls you at 7:15 pm, then it's appropriate to return their call if you are calling them back a few minutes later. But, we should not be initiating phone calls at odd times. Emails on the other hand can be sent anytime, but I would recommend keeping texts and calls between 9:00 am - 6:00 pm.

#44 - Create a Separate Phone Line for Your Business

Having a separate phone number for your business is professional. This is the number that should be on your website, Google My Business profile, vehicle wrap, etc. This is the recommended number to operate your business. Although at times it may be appropriate to share your personal cell phone with a customer depending on the job, it's best practice to have a separate line for your business for all mainstream communication. If you speak with a representative from your cell phone provider they can explain the various options to you but it's a simple process to get a local new phone number for your business.

In this chapter, we shared some nuggets on customer service. Beyond the blades of grass we cut or beautiful landscapes we install, it's a good reminder that we are serving people. And at the end of the day, the Golden Rule is a great guide to make sure we are serving our customers well. Treat others the way you want to be treated.

6

Workflow
Efficiencies

The first several chapters covered finances, sales, marketing, and customer service. In this chapter, I want to share some tactics involving workflow and executing our services with excellence and professionalism.

#45 - Make the Most of the Mornings

My friend Eric Tripplett, The Pond Digger, calls it the Timing Matrix. He explains that there are certain windows of time throughout the day when his crews are "in the zone" and get the most work done. In my experiences in the morning typically between 9:00 am - 11:00 am is when productivity is the highest point of the day.

#46 - Encourage Your Team to Pack Their Lunch

While productivity is rocking between 9:00 - 11:00 am, I also found that around lunchtime there can be a lot of wasted time. A gigantic mistake I used to make in the early years of my business is that we would eat out a lot for lunch. By eating out, I mean I would drive to Wendy's, Moe's, Subway, or Chipotle (those were the nearby restaurants) and grab lunch for the team. This would end up wasting a lot of time though. For those of you who are familiar with metro Atlanta traffic, you may understand that a simple trip to Wendy's to grab some Baconators and fries can actually take quite a while. Eventually, I realized eating out needs to be a rare treat and not a daily expectation.

As the leader of my crew, I would start to pack my own lunch and over time I was able to make it a company policy for the others to pack their lunch as well. This definitely saved time and I noticed there was more productivity leading up to our lunch break and after lunch.

#47 - Keep Your Team Hydrated

Lawn care and landscaping are hard work. One summer we had a division one college football player work with us. He was in great shape but it was rather interesting to hear from him of how difficult he thought the work was. Long days mowing, edging, blowing, and sometimes installing mulch, pine straw, flowers, plants, trees, sod, etc in the Georgia heat really is exhausting work. One basic thing to consider is keeping our team hydrated.

Do you ever watch an NFL football game? They have staff on the sidelines that as soon as a player comes off the field and even during time outs the training staff runs over and squirts some water or Gatorade through the player's helmet into the player's mouth. Now I am not suggesting hiring someone to follow your team around and squirt water into their mouth after each stripe they mow lol. But, the point is we should be mindful of how we can provide water and maybe even sports drinks to our team. One cost-effective and proven way to do this is to secure a five-gallon water jug in your vehicle or trailer. Each morning you can fill it up with ice and water and that way your team can refill their water bottles throughout the day. Some companies have a refrigerator at their shop or office that stays stocked with energy drinks, sports drinks, and water, etc.

#48 - Have a Bathroom Plan

The reality is lawn and landscaping work is done outside and on average humans typically need to use the restroom multiple times a day. Whereas you need to provide the opportunity for your team to use the restroom make sure your bathroom plan is as efficient as possible. Thankfully, in the neighborhoods we work in there has been so much construction that there are accessible portajohns nearby. I know some installation companies own or rent a porta john and bring it with them on job sites. The last thing you want to do is waste time driving to a gas station or someplace so that your team can go to the bathroom and it ends up being a huge time waster. Depending on what services you are providing and your surrounding locations, create a plan based on your route so that the bathroom breaks are as timely as possible.

Also, be careful not to let the old "I need to use the bathroom" trick put a big dent in your productivity. When you were in school did you ever request to use the hall pass to use the restroom even though you did not really need to use the restroom? Perhaps you just wanted to bust out of class and enjoy the freedom of roaming the halls. This does happen so be reasonable in providing your team the opportunities to use the restroom but also be firm that you need to stay on schedule and provide excellent service to your customers.

#49 - Clean Your Cracks

When doing lawn maintenance it's a pro move to clean the channel of your edges. For example, if you use a blade edger to edge along the sidewalk or driveway. As you are doing some finishing touch blowing at the end be sure to blow out the groove between the concrete and turf. This will help the edge look completely clean and tidy. Customers appreciate this attention to detail.

#50 - Stripe Like A Pro

My friend Blake Albertson from BB Lawn Care in Kansas City, Missouri coined the phrase "Stripe Nation." I came across Blake's YouTube videos back in 2014 and would watch Blake stripe his lawns. Those stripes were popping! How does he get those stripes to look so nice?

First and foremost it's important to understand and have realistic expectations based on what kind of turf you are cutting. For example, cool-season turf when cut at a higher height can look absolutely stunning. While it is possible to stripe warm season turf like Bermuda and Zoysia it's a lot easier to create that stunning look with cool-season turf. With that being said, how do you make the stripes and have the lawn look its best after your maintenance of a property?

The most important component is that your mower blades are sharp! Think of a morning bagel. Have you ever attempted to cut a bagel in half with a dull knife? It can be done but it's a challenge. However, if you carefully use a sharp knife, it cuts through that bagel like butter. The blades of grass are similar to the bagel. If your mower blades are dull it may get the job done, but it's not optimal. However, if your mower blades are razor-sharp then it can produce a fine cut that looks really good.

Another fundamental principle to consider is making sure you cut the turf at the proper height. There are many variables that will determine what the proper height is. What kind of turf are you cutting? Warm-season turf performs best when cut low, while cooler season turf should be higher. What month of the year is it? What are the temperatures? There is a lot to consider, but when you cut the turf with sharp blades and the accurate height you are in position for some nice results. Jeremy's team over at @JJacobsGrounds on IG creates some of the nicest stripes in the industry.

#51 - Consider Your Angles

In order to really create the most effective results when striping the grass choosing the correct angle to mow your lines at is important. The rule of thumb is to consider what view will the customer most frequently look at the lawn from? You want to make the lines go at an angle that will be in that direct view. Additionally, consider what way the street traffic flows? If you can angle your stripes so that when people drive by the property the stripes face them then it can create a very aesthetically pleasing view.

Additionally, change up your mowing pattern for each cut. This will create a good view and is also good for the turf. If you mow diagonally in one direction consider the next week mowing in the opposite direction creating a checkerboard look. Oftentimes you see this look in the outfield at Major League Baseball stadiums. Your customers will appreciate their lawn looking so good and the turf and soil will appreciate the multiple mowing patterns.

Photo credit: J. Jacobs Grounds IG @jjacobsgrounds

#52 - Sharp Mower Blades

The best practice is to start each day with each mower having a fresh set of blades. This will provide your customer with a top-notch cut. To maximize efficiency it's best that as you conclude your route each day before your team dismisses to swap out the blades. That way the next day you can hit the ground running and your lawnmowers already have sharp blades.

How do you keep the mower blades sharp? First and foremost it's good to buy them in bulk. This way you can always have backups sharp and ready to go at any moment and you can sharpen them in bulk. On YouTube, there are many videos featuring different products and methods of how to sharpen your lawnmower blades. You can literally spend hours watching these videos as various creators share the method that they find works best. I actually went on a YouTube binge one day watching these videos. At the end of the day, the reality is there are multiple ways to achieve sharp blades. I would recommend if you are going to sharpen them yourself do what you feel most comfortable with. Be very careful, it can be dangerous to sharpen the blades. It's also dangerous removing the blades from your mower and putting the new ones on. If you do not have experience doing this, in addition to watching YouTube, see if you can have a mechanic or someone at your lawnmower dealer show you the safe way to perform this service.

Lastly, another option to consider is just having a mechanic sharpen the blades for you. You can drop them off in bulk and pay a professional to sharpen them. My friend Mitchell Gordy from Mitchell's Lawn Care actually has a side hustle where he sharpens lawn mower blades in his city. Most dealers have mechanics on-site as well who can sharpen your blades for you. It will save time to sharpen them in-house, but if you want to pay someone else to do it for you it's an option. At the end of the day, be proactive to make sure you start each day with sharp blades, it really does make an important difference.

#53 - Excellent Edges

Customers appreciate clean fresh looking stripes and they also like a well-defined edge! One of the funniest stories ever told on the Green Industry Podcast is when special guest Alex Kirby from Trifecta Landscaping shared about his first lawn maintenance. He had mowed the lawn for his customer and then the customer called and asked Alex why he didn't edge? Alex, thinking on his feet, said he would be back to edge. In the meantime, he went onto good ole YouTube and started watching tutorials on how to edge. Then he went to his customer's house and edged the borders and completed the job. Alex thought he was done after mowing but quickly realized most customers' expectations for lawn maintenance is that in addition to lawn mowing you edge the borders along the driveway, sidewalk, and garden beds and then clean everything up with some finishing touch blowing to make sure everything looks neat and pristine.

Jason Creel from the Lawn Care Life on YouTube has a good video about how to edge with a weed eater or string trimmer on YouTube. Here is the link for those reading. For those of you who are listening to the Audiobook, you can just type in the video title into YouTube and it should show up. Jason's video on edging is approaching one million views.

https://www.youtube.com/watch?v=9A-eRelxYvO

My recommendation is to use a weed eater along the "soft edges" like the garden beds. As Jason shows in the video you can flip the head of the weed eater and really create a beautiful defined edge. It takes a little bit of experience but once you get it, it's like riding a bike. Although you can also use the weed eater or string trimmer along the hard edges (driveway, sidewalk, walking paths, etc) my recommendation is to use a blade edger with a sharp blade. This creates a much tighter, cleaner edge in my opinion. But, if you are going to use a weed eater or as our friends in Australia call it, a "whipper snipper," then make sure you do it carefully so you don't accidentally take a chunk out of the turf. Here is a YouTube video I made at "Geek to Freak's house, a legend in our lawncare community: https://www.youtube.com/watch?v=yjQYvCgiu-c

#54 - Be Careful Where You Refuel

Spilled gasoline will likely kill the grass. I have seen this happen one too many times. It's a good protocol to establish in your company that when refueling mowers and power equipment etc… that you always do it on a hard surface like the concrete driveway or out in the street. Obviously, you want to be careful every time and make sure you do not spill any gasoline. But, if you spill it in the grass there is little room for forgiveness. It will likely quickly get in the soil and kill the surrounding grass. There are gas cans that reduce the chances of any spills, but just to be on the safe side, refuel away from the grass.

#55 - Shoot Grass Clippings Away From Garden Beds, Driveways, and the Street

Most professional lawn maintenance companies shoot their grass clippings back into the yard. This can feed nutrients to the turf and is a whole lot more convenient than hauling the clippings to the dump. Although some customers prefer you bag the clippings. If you do have the equipment to bag the clippings make sure you factor that into your pricing.

Since most yards will get a regular mow where the clippings will shoot back into the yard, be intentional and mindful of where those clippings are going. The best practice is to start your mowing by mowing one to two borders around the property's edges shooting the clippings back into the yard. You NEVER want to shoot the clippings into the garden beds. That will create a mess. You also want to be careful not to shoot the clippings into the street or driveway. Additionally, if it's wet or the grass is super tall, you may need to double or triple cut the turf just so there are no clumps of grass resting in the yard.

#56 - Redefining the Garden Bed Edges
In the marketing chapter, I mentioned considering campaigns throughout the year for enhancing your customer's property beyond lawn mowing. Keeping the garden beds fresh with ground covers such as mulch or pine straw and some nice-looking plants and flowers goes a long way. Here in the Atlanta market, typically, the leaves fall down throughout November and December. By New Year's the vast majority of the leaves are down and the garden beds are usually about ready to be freshened up. Many companies around town will begin spreading pine straw or adding mulch throughout January and February while the grass is dormant. While some customers prefer to wait until spring, many customers are ready to see those garden beds looking better.

Whether you are adding pine straw or mulch the best practice is to also create a new redefined edge while you are working on the garden beds. For years we used shovels and sweat to trench out this new edge. The results were phenomenal. Then, I discovered the ECHO BRD 2620 Bed Redefiner! This tool works wonders. It will carve out a perfectly defined edge between the garden bed and turf. Whether you use an old-fashioned square-nosed shovel or a bed redefiner, the point is to really do your customers right and define their edge. Of course, throughout the year you can maintain the edge with your weed eater or whipper snipper, but it's good that at the same time you freshen up their garden beds you also take the time to get their edge looking as crispy as possible.

#57 - Get A Good Deal on Your Mulch

When it does come time to freshen up those garden beds I have found it works best to have the mulch delivered. Of course, if you are going to order the mulch to be delivered make sure the customer absorbs the cost of the delivery. Communicate clearly with your customer when the delivery will be made so that their vehicles will be out of the way. I like to lay down a large tarp in their driveway just so we do not stain the driveway with any of the dye from the mulch. And in regards to where to purchase the mulch from you will have to crunch the numbers in your local area. But, I found a place here in Atlanta that does tree recycling and also sells mulch. They offer a nice discount to contractors. Not only do they have the best price in town, but they also have good mulch and always deliver on time. When I was a rookie I was buying bags of mulch at the big box store or paying way too much at a local landscape yard. Eventually, I came to my senses though and found a good price from a reputable company that faithfully delivers it to my customer's house.

#58 - Tip Your Delivery Driver

Whether it's the delivery driver for your mulch, pine straw, sod, boulders or other materials always leave them a tip! The driver will appreciate this and remember you. As Caleb Auman says, "Efficiency is everything". Especially in the spring rush when the demand is through the roof, you want to make sure jobs are being completed on schedule. A factor in making sure operations are running smoothly is that the materials are being delivered on time. As your delivery drivers start to recognize your company and they know you are a good tipper they will take care of you. Take care of them financially and they will take care of you making sure your materials are delivered in a timely manner and dropped off where you want them. Make sure the material is always unloaded to the spot that sets your crew up to be as efficient as possible.

#59 - Pay Your Subcontractors and Suppliers on Time, Every Time

Piggybacking off of the principle of making sure your delivery driver is happy, you want to also make sure your suppliers and subcontractors are pleased at all times. The overall operation of a successful landscaping business is like an orchestra. In a sense, you are the conductor. We want to make sure everything is efficiently and seamlessly flowing together. While there are many components to consider in making sure our suppliers and subs are happy, making sure they are always paid up is one practical thing we can do to make sure we are in good standing with those who help make our orchestra a masterpiece.

#60 - Get The Good Pine Straw

I realize that pine straw in the garden beds is a southern thing. While most of you reading this or listening to the audiobook probably spread more mulch than pine straw, I do want to at least share a nugget about pine straw. Get the long needle pine straw! Here in Georgia they usually sell "slash" or regular pine straw. Then, they sell what we call the good stuff, the long needle pine straw. The long needle pine straw costs more but it looks way better and the color typically lasts longer. I used to offer either or to the customer, but then after getting so frustrated with the frequently poor quality of the slash pine straw began to only offer the long needle. Having my customers' yards look nice is more important to me than saving them a few bucks on less quality material. Not all pine straw is the same, the long needle is better.

#61 - Learn From A Mentor How To Properly Plant

While mowing grass and spreading mulch is relatively simple, planting flowers, plants and trees have a little more of a learning curve in my opinion. In my first book *Cut That Grass and Make That Cash* I mentioned how during my first few months in the business I was mowing with my buddy Tyler. Thankfully, Tyler's mom is a Georgia Certified Landscape Professional and early on she was able to teach me the ropes with planting. She taught me the basics of how deep to dig the holes, how to space out the area between plants, and taught me some main design concepts that would help me to confidently sell garden bed designs to customers.

I was able to teach myself with experience and by watching YouTube videos how to mow, edge, trim and blow. But, it really was helpful to have a hands-on mentor teach me how to plant like a pro. I understand it was a rare set of circumstances that my friend's mom just so happened to be a certified landscape professional who was willing to take the time to train me on the proper way to install flowers, plants, and trees. But there are other ways you can expedite your training so that you and your team can offer enhancements to your customers.

#62 - Explore Your County Extension Offices Training Programs

Here in Georgia, our county extension offices have incredible training opportunities. You will have to look into what's offered in your neck of the woods but here in Georgia, we are blessed with the programs available. The UGA Extension provides advice about caring for and protecting lawns and landscapes from pests and disease and helps both homeowners and lawn care professionals ensure that their grass is always greener. I personally have taken multiple courses from them, the price was only $20 for an eight-hour training! I have learned much from highly educated instructors from the University of Georgia for only $20 a pop. They offer a wide variety of training throughout the year. Some of the classes teach how to count your overhead and correctly set your prices while others go over identifying weeds and they cover pretty much anything and everything in between! It's excellent teaching at a very affordable price.

7

Sod Best Practices

I absolutely love installing fresh sod. It's one of those jobs that when you are done - it instantly transforms a property. As time rolls on my two favorite landscaping services are installing sod and reel mowing turf. The entrepreneur in me wants to start a sod company. The riches are in the niches and I often contemplated owning a company that only installs sod. I've had similar thoughts of starting a lawn mowing company that only reel mows properties. In this chapter my goal is to share about my passion for sod and if you choose to offer this service how you can do it with excellence.

#63 - Carefully Calculate the Square Footage

At one of the UGA Extension office classes I took, they gave us the assignment to measure the square footage of irregular areas. The class was full of landscape professionals and shockingly we just about all had different answers! Only one person got the actual correct answer. The rest of us were off. Some off by a little, and some by a lot. Measuring the square footage of a square or rectangle is rather simple but when the area is irregular it takes being careful. If you didn't pay attention in math class and forget how to discover the square footage of an area that's ok. There is plenty of examples and step-by-step tutorials online that will teach you how to do it. But as you measure and calculate, measure twice! Make sure your count is accurate. I have made multiple measuring mistakes and have both ordered too little sod and too much sod. You want to make sure you have the exact measurement and then order just a little extra sod because as you carve out your borders and create curves around the garden beds you will "lose" some sod so I always order a little extra. The main point though is to get accurate with your measuring so you are ordering the proper amount of sod.

#64 - Grade Like The Pros

One of the key components to installing sod is to first make sure you have a perfect grade. There are multiple paths to take to create the proper grade in preparation for a sod installation. Some go tos are using a machine like the Toro Dingo with the soil cultivator attachment or a skid steer with the bucket. Although I do not recommend it, you can actually use a strong rototiller and landscape rakes.

In my Chuck in the Truck days when I was starting out in the lawn care business that's all I could afford to do. I would go to Home Depot and rent the rototiller for the day and till up the area where we were about to lay the sod. A common issue in Georgia is that years ago folks planted Bermuda sod, but over time the Bermuda got stressed or even died because it was under canopies of trees and did not receive enough sunlight. Customers would then have the dead or stressed Bermuda replaced with Zoysia sod that requires less sunlight. We typically would limb up the surrounding trees as well to ensure the Zoysia thrives.

Anyway, money was tight and I did not have a skid steer or mini skid steer and so I would just rent a rototiller for the day. That machine is a workout! Wow! You will sleep well after operating all day. After the soil was tilled up, then I would rake out all the grass, weeds, twigs, debris and haul it off to the dump. After that, I would use a landscape rake along with a concrete grader tool to smooth out the soil slowly working the slope away from the house. This method will get the job done on a budget but there are more efficient ways of doing it.

Eventually, I started subcontracting out the grading to my buddy Joe. He owns a grading company and for a very reasonable rate would come and grade the area with his skid steer, he would haul off all the debris and then bring back a fresh load of screened topsoil and grade the area to near perfection. Next, I will use the landscape rake to finish things up and make sure the grade is smooth.

Joe cut me a great deal, but best practice is probably to just use a mini skid steer and the soil cultivator attachment. Depending on what's near you there likely is a place where you can rent a Toro, Ditch Witch, or Vermeer mini skid for the day with the proper attachment. Just let them know you are grading for sod and they can get you set up. The goal with the grading is to make sure everything is smooth and prepped for the sod. And of course, know your numbers! The grading and preparing for the sod installation is a lot of work even if you use the proper equipment and you want to make sure you fully calculate that into your price for the job.

#65 - Select The Proper Turf When Installing Sod

It took me years but finally, I found a sod supplier in Atlanta who has the heart of a teacher. For a while, I was using another company but they would talk down to me when I was a rookie and I am really thankful to eventually find a supplier who took the time to really educate me about sod. Of course, I used common sense and relational intelligence and did not bother them with all my questions when they were slammed with customers. But, on days when they were slow, I would pick their brains about turf. Not all grass is the same. For example here in Georgia we predominantly have Zoysia and Bermuda sod. But, even though they are both warm-season turfs, they have a lot of differences. On top of that, there are multiple variations of each. It can get complex! But the good news is your sod supplier can be a great resource to help you understand what performs best in your area. Thoroughly understanding the different types of turfs in your region and what performs best will help you sell the right type of sod to your customer and help the lawn look great.

#66 - Position The Pallets For Maximum Efficiency

Previously I suggested tipping your delivery drivers. When the sod delivery driver sees me he has a big smile! He knows he is going to get a nice tip. I take good care of him because he can save us a ton of time by placing the pallets in strategic locations so that we can lay the sod as efficiently as possible. A lazy delivery driver may attempt to just drop all your pallets off in the street or driveway. But, I always request the driver to use the forklift and place the pallets where I direct him to. This way once we start laying the sod we don't have to spend any extra time transporting it because it's conveniently located near where it's about to be laid.

#67 - Stagger Sod Like Bricks

When it comes time to lay the sod you want to lay it like bricks so that the seems are staggered. This will prevent drainage issues and help the turf to fill in nicely. Additionally, make sure the pieces or rolls of sod are very tight. I get aggressive and really jam the pieces or rolls together and make sure there are no gaps or air pockets.

#68 - Roll The Sod When You Are Done

After all of the sod is laid and your borders are beautifully carved out with a machete roll the sod! The sod roller will really help to press down the roots and help them to connect with the soil and remove any air pockets. Make sure the sod roller is full of water and slowly go over the sod. This step is really important and makes a big difference.

#69 - Give The Customer Clear Watering Instructions

The school of experience has taught me a lot! One of those valuable lessons is to make sure the customer has clear instructions on how frequently to water the sod after it's installed. The sod supplier should have this information based on the temperatures and season of the year. But you want to make sure your customer understands the significance of making sure the sod properly gets water until it fully takes root and is established. Basically, once that sod is cut at the sod farm it's in survival mode fighting for its life. It needs water, air, and sun to live. Depending on the temperatures it can last a little while without water but if it goes too long without water it will die. I have seen it happen time and time again. So make sure your customer knows how urgent it is to water the sod. And I would recommend not giving any guarantee because you don't know if they will water it and you should not be responsible to replace the sod because they fail to water it. I learned this one the hard way. Here's the story.

After installing sod for one customer they referred their friend to me. This prospective customer called me and I walked over to the property with him and swiftly delivered a quote to plant some new flowers, plants, and trees in their garden beds and put fresh new Zoysia sod in both the front and back yard. I quoted him $14,000 for the job. In hindsight, this was way underpriced, but at the moment I was a complete rookie.

Before the customer cut me the deposit check he expressed his concern about the new Zoysia not taking root and so he asked me if I would guarantee the work. This intimidated me a little, but after talking to the sod farm they assured me if it was properly watered it should take root. And so being young and dumb I told the customer, no problem, the sod will be guaranteed and I even went above and beyond and told him that it's a one-year guarantee! If any of the turf does not look good that first year I will replace it.

This job ended up taking a lot longer than anticipated. I failed to calculate how difficult it would be to transport the sod to the backyard. It took about five pallets in the backyard and because there was no path to get back there other than steep stone steps, we had to individually walk each roll of sod to the back. Talk about back-breaking work. It rained the day we did the installation so just imagine walking five pallets of heavy rolls of sod down slippery stone stairs. Not fun.

Eventually, though, we got the job done. After rolling the sod, it looked very nice. Ten pallets of Zoysia. All the new plants and trees we installed were looking superb and we freshened up the mulch throughout the entire large property. The customer seemed happy and paid me the final payment for the project. After running all my calculations, I was dismayed to realize I barely made money on this job. It took longer than I assumed and cost more in materials and labor than I forecasted. Not to mention we worked in rainy conditions. If the story ended here, however, it would have obviously not made it in the book.

About a month later in Georgia, the warm season turfs transition into dormancy. For those folks who live where there is cool-season turf, in the late fall and winter months grass changes from green to tan. And so throughout the winter, this sod appeared tan just like all the other neighboring lawns. Even though I was a rookie, I could suspect that this sod was not looking too healthy. It felt kind of crispy but since it looked identical to the other lawns in the neighborhood. I was hoping for the best, that it would resurrect and spring up to a lush green first of spring.

Winter had come and gone and the next thing you know, it was springtime in Georgia. Typically, in April and certainly in May the lawns start greening up depending on multiple conditions such as how much nitrogen fertilizer you put out. This is about the time my phone started blowing up. The customer for whom we installed the ten pallets of Zoysia told me his grass was still "brown." He reminded me that I would replace it if he was not happy and said he was not happy and requested I replace it. My response was let's give it a week or so and see if it greens up. And so we waited and nothing happened. It was not dormant as I hoped. It was dead!

The customer did not properly water the sod, that is why it's dead and here I am now having to replace it. I had foolishly given him my word that I would guarantee the work and so I got to work ripping out the sod in the front and back yard and hauling it all to the dump. Then, re-grading the area and installing new sod. At this point, I realized I had lost thousands of dollars on this job. In addition to that, I was missing out on other work. It was the middle of the spring rush, my phone was ringing off the hook, but I was out on this job replacing the sod that we installed months prior.

Talk about frustrating. As I dripped in sweat, I was so upset, but in that pain, I made a decision I would never guarantee installations again. Not because I ever looked to cut a corner or not do a good job. But, because I could not control all the variables and we are dealing with living organisms. What if the customer does not water the sod or plants and it dies? Why should I then pay to cover for their negligence? Anyway, I thought I had learned a valuable lesson in the school of experience through this oversight.

The summer rolled on and I was working long hard days. We also had a historic drought that summer. The temperatures were in the 90s day after day and we had not had a drop of rain. This is when the unthinkable happened! The same customer calls me back up, furious. In a very animated way, he explained that his grass had died again and he demanded I come and replace it, again! Now, this time I knew for sure why it did not make it. He did not water it enough! I would drive by in the mornings and notice he was not watering the sod adequately. I would even encourage him to water more. Nevertheless, with the drought conditions, the new sod had not made it for a second time.

The customer was absolutely livid and kept threatening me with my guarantee. Emotionally I was at wit's end. I had all these other folks calling me offering work. And here is this previous customer wanting me to come sod his yard for the third time. The caveat was my foolish mistake to guarantee the work. And so I drove over to the sod supplier and shared the situation with them. I showed them the pictures from both the first and second time we installed the sod. It was lush green and looked very nice both times. They reassured me that I did everything properly and the sod was healthy and well when we put it down. The reason it did not make it was plain and simple, a lack of water.

After explaining this to the customer, he did not want to hear it. He instructed me to re-sod it again. Talk about being in between a rock and a hard place. As a young business owner, this was an overwhelming situation for me. Here I was spending thousands upon thousands of dollars on material and labor for a job we were deep in the red on. All meanwhile, turning away additional work because I was wrapped up in this job. The good news though was it was really really teaching me some valuable lessons. As I was out there a third time, walking those heavy rolls of sod to the backyard I really was determined to never let this ever happen again in the future. This work was way too exhausting to lose money on a job. I'll never forget being in that backyard on my hands and knees putting in those last few rolls of sod. I felt so defeated, but little did I know I was being trained to establish boundaries so that I did not repeat this mistake ever again.

After that third and final time installing the sod, I was very bold with the customer letting him know the sod is healthy, perfect and it was on him to water it. He did and to this day that yard looks fantastic. In hindsight, I should have never accepted that job, I was still too inexperienced and did not have my efficiencies or pricing dialed in yet. In addition to that, I learned not to ever guarantee work. The temperatures are too hot here and if a customer skips out on watering the trees, plants, or sod they will surely die and that needs to be on the customer, not me. And from that moment on I never guaranteed installation again. I would give the customer very detailed water recommendations that the sod supplier provided. I would always take pictures immediately after installation to prove that what we put in was healthy and well and now the ball is in the customer's court to be responsible for properly watering the sod.

8

The Big Costs of the Little Extras

Once you establish your company's goals and blueprint it's important to execute that plan. Mike Tyson famously said, "Everyone has a plan until they get punched in the mouth." In business, we are often dealt some punches, but a lot of times they could have and should have been avoided if we stayed in our lane.

#70 - Learn to Say NO!

The following story is a classic example of a lesson I learned through the school of experience as I bit off more than I could chew.

At the onset of my landscaping business, I also had a part-time job at a restaurant. Word quickly spread amongst the staff of my side hustle to cut that grass and make that cash. One day the owner of the restaurant called me aside. I kind of felt like it was a trip to the principal's office. Was I in trouble? Thankfully, I was not. The owner mentioned that he heard I had a lawn care business. He asked me if I could come and haul away a bunch of debris that was piled up in his backyard and clean up the rest of the yard. He explained that in previous years he would burn the pile. But, because we were in the drought there was a county ordinance that burning debris was prohibited. He had a mower and would occasionally mow, but he also needed me to edge and tidy up the place.

At this point in my business, no was not a part of my vocabulary. I told the owner I would be happy to haul away his debris and clean up the property. I quoted him $300. He agreed on the price and we scheduled the job for a morning later that week.

At the time my schedule was overbooked. I was burning the candle at both ends. I immediately regretted taking on this job, because I had a bunch of other lawns to attend to and had limited time because most evenings I needed to be at the restaurant by 4:00 PM. As a solution, I asked my co-worker at the restaurant Carmello if he would help me with the job. I told him we could split it 50/50. $150 for him, $150 for me. He drove a van and said he could help and suggested we bag up the debris in large heavy-duty trash bags. He could fit a lot in his van. We were the classic Chuck in the Truck and Stan in the Van.

We got started on the job shortly after sunrise. Everything was off to a great start. We were quickly bagging up the debris and loading them into the van. I was thinking, this seems too good to be true. We are about to make $300 in a very short amount of time. I was calculating that I would work a whole long tiring shift at the restaurant and probably not make $150. And here in a short few hours was about to bank $150. This is good money I thought.

That's when the customer, who is the owner of the restaurant, came out. He buttered us up with some ice-cold drinks and complimented us on how great of a job we were doing. That's when he hit us by asking for a quick favor. As we were completing the clean-up with finishing touch blowing, he noticed we had a blower on his property. He asked us, "Hey guys since you got that blower here do you mind-blowing out the gutters real quick? I'll throw in an extra $50. The leaves get in there and since you're here it would be nice if you could blow out the gutters real quick."

Carmello and I looked at each other. We were both thinking (NO!) but both reluctantly nodded and said sure we can do that. As the customer went to his garage to grab his ladder Carmello and I devised a plan. I shared with Carmello that I don't like heights so he said he would get on the roof if I would at least bring him up the blower. And that's what we did.

We successfully got the ladder set up. Carmello got up on the roof and I followed him and handed off the blower. He got to work and the dry leaves seemed to be flying out of the gutter. Carmello swung around to the front of the house and was dominating those leaves. As he was up there blowing I noticed a brand new Cadillac Escalade slowly pull in the driveway. A lady gets out and asks me if I am the owner of the lawn care business. I said yes.

She pointed to her house that was down the road. She said she had a lot of leaves in her gutter and asked if we could blow out her gutters too. Since we were having a great time that morning, I told her "Yes!" It wasn't even noon and I figured Carmello and myself could make a little extra. As she was asking the price, I could hear Carmello who was still on the roof now in the back of the house screaming my name. I knew it was serious and so I told the neighbor lady I will be right back.

I curiously walked into the backyard and as I turned the corner I saw the ladder had broken the window to the house and half the ladder was in the house and the other half was sticking out the broken window, hanging in mid-air. That's when the restaurant owner walked out cussing up a storm. Carmelo was stuck on the roof. Then, the lady walked through the back gate and assessed the scene. As I looked at her she said, "Well sir on second thought, I'll pass" and then she walked off in disbelief.

My heart sunk in my chest. There was glass from the window everywhere. It was on the floor in the house and in the yard. The restaurant owner then pointed to the large dark clouds in the sky. He energetically encouraged us to do something because it was about to rain in his house.

I pulled the ladder out of his house and set it up against the house so Carmelo could come down from the roof. Then, I called my neighbor who I knew was a handyman. He said he could come and fix the window. He said it would be a $250 deposit when he showed up. Then, I would have to pay him for the repair. I told him to come and fix it.

Thankfully, he showed up within about an hour. I paid him the $250 deposit and then he went and bought the correct size window and came back and replaced it. Thankfully, and miraculously in the meantime, it did not rain. The dark clouds seemed to be all around us but somehow the precipitation never came. I ended up paying $550 for the window repair and Carmelo and I were the butt of many jokes at the restaurant.

In summary, this was another job in the red. I wasted my time, lost money, and hurt my reputation. The neighbor that was inquiring about gutter cleaning her house retracted her request and the restaurant owner never asked me to work on his property again and obviously did not refer me to any of his friends or neighbors. The good that came of this experience though was that it taught me some more valuable lessons.

One takeaway was that I was realizing that I was offering too many services. The customer had a need for gutter cleaning and I let his need drive my decision-making. It would have been different if I actually strategized and planned to offer gutter cleaning services. And had the right safety, equipment, and pricing for those services. But, I did not. The customer dictated the price and we, like rookies, used his equipment to do the job. This scenario was teaching me to start to clarify what services I offer and what ones I don't. It also was reminding me to rinse and repeat what I was profitable and skilled at performing.

At that time, lawn maintenance was my bread and butter. Even though in our industry lawn mowing may be the least profitable compared to jobs like retaining walls and stone patio pavers etc. Because I was getting very efficient with mowing, edging, and blowing, it was my most profitable service. I was confident I could make someone's grass look nice because I kept my lawnmower blades super sharp. And I also did a meticulous job with the edger and weed eater around the driveway, sidewalk, and garden beds. It was like art to me, making the property look as immaculate as possible. My customers were continuously complimenting me for how I made their lawn look and I actually enjoyed doing maintenance. I had a genuine love for the lawn. But, I realized I was getting myself in trouble when I was doing all these extras like gutter cleaning in which I was not experienced. At the end of the day, it taught me to develop clarity of what services to offer and what not to offer. And it taught me to take control of my schedule. In order to have margin in my life and business, I could not keep saying yes to 100% of the inquiries that came in. I need to learn how to vet and learn how to politely and professionally tell people "NO", when applicable.

#71 - Have a Plan of How You Handle Gutter Cleaning

The story of the ladder shattering Fred's window has many lessons hidden amongst the humor. One of those is to truly have a plan of how you are to handle your customers' requests to clean their gutters. For me, it was a trifecta that led me to halt all gutter cleaning services. The traumatizing experience at Fred's house was one reason. Secondly, I am afraid of heights. And third, around the same time as Fred's job I had a friend Mickey fall off a roof. Thankfully he landed in a bush and was able to survive the fall.

Long story short I realized my wheelhouse was on the ground in the yard not up on the roof.

If you are going to provide gutter cleaning or even install Christmas lights, make sure to talk with your insurance agent and have the necessary coverage to protect your company as you perform these types of services. And if you are like me and prefer not to clean gutters, that's okay! It's okay to tell your customers no. As we frequently say on the Green Industry Podcast, when you are clear on what you want to say yes to, then you can have the courage and clarity to know what to say no to.

9

Tools for the Trade

Equipment, software, and technology have all come a long way since I started my lawn business in the spring of 2011. There are many great opportunities to really increase efficiency in our operations by utilizing the necessary tools available.

#72 - Purchase Reliable Power Equipment

Does it really take money to make money? Having quality, durable and reliable power equipment should be very high on your priority list. In the long run, investing in good power equipment has many benefits. I understand if you are in that broke, busted, and disgusted season of life that duct-taping together old equipment is sometimes what needs to be done. However, as soon as possible you need to update to solid dependable power equipment. If you are doing lawn maintenance, having strong weed eaters, stick edgers, hedge trimmers, and blowers is essential. Do whatever it takes (legally) to scrape the funds together to have a good lineup of power equipment.

#73 - Have Backup Equipment

When you are just getting started and perhaps funds are limited and tight then this tip may be a long-term play. But, nevertheless, it is important to eventually have backups and reserves for your vehicles, trailers, mowers, equipment, and parts, etc... Recently, I was watching some IG stories where I came across an interesting post from my friend Joshua Sutton of Sutton Outdoors. Josh was holding up a little $1.88 part he bought at the big box store and he was emphasizing that this little two-dollar part actually cost him over $60? He explained that he needed the part to get his machine back up and running so he could complete the work for his customer. But, he did not have the part in his truck or at his nearby shop. So Josh had to stop his workflow, drive to the big box store, look for the part, wait in line and eventually get back to the job site, fix the machine, and get back to work. Josh in his wisdom reminded those watching on IG to have backups!! If he would have had the part nearby he could have done the repair in minutes, but rather it took him over an hour to travel to the store and back to get the part. With his rate of at least $60 per man hour, he explained how the part really cost him over $60 when calculating his time to go buy the part during the heart of working hours. This happens far too often in our industry.

#74 - Purchase Edger Blades In Bulk

I am a big fan of stick edgers. I love the way they define the edge along the driveway, walk path, and sidewalks. What I don't like though is when the once large sharp stick edger blade dwindles down to a nub. Swapping stick edger blades out is super simple once you get the hang of it. Therefore, having blades available at all times is vital. They sell them in 50 packs and it's smart to stock up and always have them handy.

#75 - Capitalize on the Good Deals

Throughout the year there are some good days to shop and save big on equipment and parts etc… It will take a little research in your market but be aware that there are good deals to be had. Taking advantage of these deals can be a cost savings way to make sure you have the proper tools for the trade and the necessary backups so that you are not repeating Josh's mistake and making an unnecessary run to the big box store.

Our friends here in Atlanta at Howard Brothers have their annual Pro day. This is typically in February and they offer big savings. This is a good time to buy those stick edger blades, lawnmower blades, and other backup parts in bulk. You save money by making the purchase on a day when you get an additional discount and you save time in the future when you already have the parts "in stock" at your shop or in your trailer.

#76 - Take Good Care of Your Mechanic

By staying diligent with the necessary maintenance on vehicles, mowers, and equipment, hopefully, repairs are minimized. The reality is though sometimes vehicles, mowers, and our equipment need to be fixed. If you have the knowledge and time to make the repairs "in-house" it can be wise, but sometimes it's more profitable in the long run to let a professional mechanic get the job done.

There are a lot of crooks out there. I found out the hard way. Step one is to find a reputable, honest, good mechanic. These may be separate people. Perhaps one for your vehicles, one for your mowers, one for your power equipment, etc… But when you find a good one, make sure you take good care of them.

#77 - Stay on Top of Proper Maintenance

Have you ever heard the ancient saying, "an apple a day keeps the doctor away"? The point is if you feed your body with good nutrition you are setting yourself up for fewer visits to the doctor. It's a similar principle to taking care of our equipment. A pro move I learned from Caleb Auman is to write down on various equipment when you last changed the oil and perform various other work. For example, if you have a skid steer, keep a sharpie nearby, and somewhere on the machine keep a repair log. This works for our vehicles and various equipment. By keeping current logs we should be alert and in the know of when it's time to change the oil and complete other recommended maintenance.

#78 - Protect Your Equipment

Paul Capote, the Miami Landscaper shared one of the most shocking stories on the Green Industry Podcast. Paul was out running errands his foreman called him and asked where the truck and trailer were. Paul thought it was a joke and replied it's sitting in front of the customer's house. But, the foreman reiterated to Paul it was not!

Long story short, while Paul's crew was in the backyard some thieves came and stole the Miami Landscapers truck and trailer. On the trailer was Paul's brand new Wright Stander mower! In one swipe these thieves stole Paul's truck, trailer, and new mower. Unfortunately, Paul was not properly insured.

Now, the good news is later the vehicle was found but this was a sobering reminder that we must proactively protect our equipment. One way we can protect our equipment is to make sure it's insured. A simple call with your insurance broker and they can share the various policies to consider.

Where you store your company's equipment and tools is also important. I have heard countless stories of thieves making their moves at night. Even though a lot of these heartbreaking moments are caught on surveillance often the thieves don't get caught and the landscape company is out whatever was stolen. The best practice is to research and consider where is the safest place to store your stuff overnight.

#79 - Protect Your Team

Annually there are way too many lawn and landscape deaths and injuries. One year in the same neighborhood that we provide service in, a lawn care professional passed away after the mower flipped over and landed on him as he was mowing a slope. Jeremiah Jennings shared on the Green Industry Podcast of his hand injury when his hand got sliced by his hedge clippers. How do we protect our team and surroundings when operating such potentially dangerous equipment and machines? Personal Protective Equipment (PPE) is a great place to start. It varies based on what work you are doing, but some of the most common basics to consider are eye, ear, hand, and foot protection. Another typical PPE to consider is chaps and protective headgear for chainsaw work and a harness for anything above six feet above the lower level. Additionally, using high visibility features on your vests, hats, apparel, and vehicles can help keep your team safe. Lastly, high visibility cones can be very helpful and in many situations are required by law.

10

Business Development and Networking

#80 - Surround Yourself With People Smarter Than You

Jim Rohn shares that we are the average of the five people we spend the most time with. Who and what is influencing you? People, music, podcasts, videos, social media news feeds, all influence the way we think. Our ears and eyes are essentially gates to our thoughts. What we allow to enter into us through our eyes and ears will ultimately affect the future decisions we make.

Who is influencing your life and business? Are they pulling you higher into the greatness of your destiny? Or are they dragging you down and sucking the life out of you? It's essential to frequently take inventory of how we are being influenced. If we want different results we may need to change and adjust who and what is influencing us.

Interestingly enough when my business really started to excel to the next level is when I started hanging around three of my mentors Jamie, Rich, and Kenny. Each of them owned their own landscaping business. Jamie does design and build, Kenny does lawn maintenance and landscaping and Rich specializes in lighting and irrigation. They are all above 50 years old and have decades of experience in the industry.

Many times I would see them in person because they worked in the same area. Whether it was at a nursery or out in the field anytime I could engage them in a conversation I would. Frequently I will text or call them just to pick their brain about business. Their intellect, experiences, and knowledge helped guide me to success.

With modern technology and communication, we also have incredible opportunities to network and grow in ways that transcend geographical location. Caleb Auman from the Kid Contractor Podcast and Naylor Taliaferro from the LCR Media podcast are two of my best friends. Truth be told, years before any of us had podcasts we were already friends and consistently communicating with each other in a group chat. We would message each other back and forth discussing how we can improve our businesses and take our lives to the next level. Iron sharpening iron. If you really want your life and business to reach their fullest potential be very calculated with whom and what is influencing you. Surround yourself with those you aspire to be like.

#81 - Attend In-Person Training Programs and Events

Previously I mentioned the incredible opportunity we have in the state of Georgia with the affordable high-value training opportunities assembled by the county extension office and the University of Georgia. While I understand the majority of those reading and listening to this may not have that opportunity, there are still many other training programs and events to consider attending throughout the year to help you network and gain the knowledge to help improve your business and life.

A few of these events to consider is the Kohler Engines event. This typically takes place in February in Hattiesburg, Mississippi, and is full of business training and networking opportunities. Then generally in the summer, there is the Together in the Trades summit. This is hosted by my friends Brian and Liz Fullerton and Caleb and Brittany Auman. It's in a different city each year and is designed for couples in business who want to thrive not just in their business but also in their marriage and family. Then in the fall is the Lawntrepreneur Academy Live event in Novi, Michigan. This is an all-day training event full of motivation, networking, and knowledge to help you grow your business.

#82 - Consider Attending the Equip Exposition

The "Super Bowl" for the Green Industry is annually in October in Louisville, Kentucky aka the Equip Exposition! This is a trade show that features the latest and greatest products in the industry and also is an incredible opportunity to network with others in the industry.

#83 - Network with Your Dealer and Supplier

Where do you purchase the equipment and materials for your business? While some things may be ordered online and conveniently delivered to your doorstep, more than likely other items are still bought at a local dealer or supplier. Behind the products and materials that we purchase to operate our business are people! Taking the time to be kind and get to know these folks has been a huge blessing to my life and business.

For example, Martin from our local nursery has been a huge help. Early on when I was very new at understanding designing and installing landscapes I would often go into the nursery with a picture of my customer's house and tell Martin about the project. He will analyze the house and landscape and help me with some ideas of how we can turn it into a masterpiece. Then, I would price out the project, send off the quote, and more times than not land the job. We would do a bang-out job and our customers were thankful. The reality was that Martin was integral to my success.

How did I get connected with Martin and why was he so willing to help a rookie? To bring this full circle, I mentioned my mentor Jamie earlier in the chapter. Jamie's business was a big-time customer at Martin's nursery. Long story short, Jamie introduced me to Martin and his staff. That key relationship gave me instant credibility with Martin. Since Jamie was a "big fish" he wanted to keep her happy and so that more than likely influenced him to be so generous and helpful to me. In addition to that, I quickly established rapport with Martin. He loves football and his Tennessee Volunteers, and so I would chat with him about that and we became friends.

In most of my books, the stories I share are of failure and what I learned from my mistakes. This story of how Martin helped me crush landscaping jobs, is actually a story of something I was able to do right. I share the story to encourage you to be mindful that the folks where you buy your products and materials can be a big asset to your business. Be kind to them and in an organic natural way build healthy relationships with them.

11

Becoming a Better Leader

#84 - Express Gratitude to Your Team

Have you ever felt taken for granted or underappreciated? It does not feel good. Back in the day, I had a couple of bosses at previous jobs that never seemed to notice when I did a good job, but one little misstep and I was sure to hear about it. Although at the time that was frustrating it helped teach me a valuable leadership lesson and that is to let others know you appreciate them. Expressing thanks, gratitude and appreciation are very attractive. Whether it's an employee, subcontractor, peer, supplier, or even customer we can never say thank you too much.

#85 - Lead by Example

It has been said that "talk is cheap" and that actions "speak louder than words." A hypocrite is a person who pretends to have virtues, moral or religious beliefs, principles, etc., that he or she does not actually possess. If you say one thing yet do another the consequence is those around you will take notice and will lose respect for you and trust in you.

Over the years I have seen this first hand in various companies and organizations. "On paper" there is a set of guiding principles and beliefs, but in private, the leaders live contrary to what they publicly proclaim. One of the greatest attributes of quality leaders is that who they are and what they say in private matches who they are and what they say in public.

#86 - Have an Accountability Partner

As business leaders, we are responsible for a lot. Our decisions influence many people whether we realize it or not. From our customers to our team members and their families and many others. We affect other people's lives. Having an accountability partner or even accountability partners who have access to our lives and can correct us when necessary is a best practice from many leaders who actually have integrity and lasting success.

The impeccable character of Billy Graham has taught me a lot about leadership. Billy led a large organization that annually brought in hundreds of millions of dollars of revenue. He managed a lot of money and people. As an itinerant evangelist month after month, he was speaking his message of hope to large crowds in stadiums and arenas across the world. He died at a good old age of 99, living from 1918 - 2018. His influence exploded in the 1950s and for well over 60 years his life was within the limelight.

What impressed me about Billy's life and leadership skills was the great intentionality he invested into making sure his character was excellent. Not once did you ever hear about a scandal involving Billy Graham. Although his enemies and the peanut gallery plotted and schemed to make him fail and stumble, Billy consistently made good decisions. He practiced what he preached.

As lawn and landscape business leaders we may not influence as many folks as a public figure like Billy Graham did. But we can learn a lot about how he successfully led his tribe and earned the trust and respect of his followers and team. What was his formula for leadership success?

One of the main components was accountability. At the beginning of his career, Billy set a team around him consisting of a few men of character that would hold him accountable for his actions, specifically how he handles money and his relationship with women. Billy remained faithful to his wife throughout all the years of travel, riches, and fame and stewarded the money with integrity. Having wise boundaries and an accountability team helped keep Dr. Graham on the straight and narrow. Prioritizing having excellent character is important in our efforts to become a great leader. None of us are perfect. We all have made enough mistakes in our lives to feel disqualified from leading a business. But, thankfully there is grace that we can get back up and try again. Let's not take for granted that we have fresh new opportunities to get things right and be men and women of exceptional character.

#87 - Be Intentional To Build Trust with Customers and Your Team

People do business with people they know, like, and trust. Trust takes time to build and can be broken in an instant. One of the main threads that are consistently shared by guests on the Green Industry Podcast is how beneficial word-of-mouth referrals are. On the flip side of this neighbors and friends also share about companies to be wary of or avoid. People love to talk and share their experiences whether good, bad, or ugly. Therefore, do the right thing, build trust, be likable and reap the rewards of having a good reputation in the industry and in your community.

#88 - Become The Expert

I have mentioned my mentor and friend Jamie a lot in this book because her company truly does the finest work I have ever seen. I often stand back and just gaze in amazement at how great her team makes properties look with their installations. It's beautiful work. And needless to say, Jamie's phone is ringing off the hook with people trying to hire her to come and spruce up their properties. She is trustworthy not just because of her and her team's character. But, she is trustworthy because she is an expert and her team does phenomenal work.

There have been so many late nights when Jamie was up studying and learning. In Georgia, she passed the ultimate exam becoming a Georgia Certified Landscape Professional. And she is continuously studying and staying on top of industry news, trends and opportunities.

There is a big difference between just doing the bare minimum of enough to get by versus being a top expert in a field. Of course, we do not arrive overnight at rock star status knowing it all. But, I challenge you to train your leaders and team to be experts who are knowledgeable and skilled at the services you provide.

#89 - Build A Business That Has A Purpose Greater Than Profit

John Mackay said, "Just as people cannot live without eating, so a business cannot live without profits. But most people don't live to eat, and neither must businesses live just to make profits." Profit in our businesses is needed for lasting success. But profit alone is not the end all be all. There must be a greater purpose for our companies. Andy Mulder from Mulder Outdoor Services has caught a vision of this and I hope his passion for his family contagiously spreads to influence others in our industry.

#90 - Dadurday

I wrote quite a bit about Andy Mulder in chapter four of my previous book *Best Business Practices for Landscapers.* Andy is a leader I deeply respect. As host of the Green Industry Podcast, I have been blessed to have been able to spend some quality time in person with him and he is an absolutely great guy and solid role model for our industry.

Andy's work ethic is matchless. Not that it's necessary to run a successful business, but he chooses to be a laborer in his business as he daily works in the field with his team. Andy has worked very hard building his company for years and has experienced tremendous success. The business is profitable, his mortgage on his home is paid off and he is completely debt-free not to mention he has quite a bit of money saved up. What's impressive about Andy's business though is not just the financial success and breathtaking gallery of work his team has performed over the years.

Andy is intentional to spend time with his family and make them a priority in his life. Specifically, Andy makes arrangements so that he is available on Saturdays to spend quality time with his children. This is an extraordinary example of great leadership by Andy Mulder.

12

Making the Most of the Offseason

#91 - Have a Profitable Plan For Your Wintertime

The offseason is a very interesting time. Depending on what part of the world you live in, the recommended strategies for what to do in the winter months vary. Some folks do Christmas lights, others plow that snow and make that dough, some do installations and others like Johnny Mow save up enough money during the season and enjoy several weeks off before ramping back up for the spring rush. There are lots of options and a huge variable is your geographical location and weather.

While the folks up north may turn to plowing that snow and making that dough in these winter months. The white gold just doesn't fall in the south. Perhaps, occasionally we may get a blizzard, aka, 1-3 inches, but that is rare and most years it never even snows. All that's really left to do is pruning and tree services. Most companies here in Atlanta will use this time to limb up the canopies on the trees throughout the property as well as do any specialty pruning. Additionally, some companies offer holiday lighting. Although the installation of these holiday lights will occur in October or November, the removal of these lights can happen in January. Then, last but not least, it's pine straw time! With all the leaves down, it is a good time to freshen up the garden beds with some pine straw or mulch. There are a few customers who will want to wait until spring, but most are accommodating and will welcome some fresh pine straw or mulch to kick off the year. For those in much of the South, you know these months fly by. Once you have the properties pruned and the garden beds freshened up, the next thing you know it's the beginning of March, and time to scalp the warm season grass. Even though the grass is dormant, it's nice to cut it as low as you can go early March and start the season with the turf nice and low. After that, the spring rush hits and you are off to the races.

Although snow removal can be profitable if you do it right and have consistent snowfall. It can also be a money-sucking pit if you are not careful. The most dangerous regions are those right on the border of the transitional zones throughout Virginia, West Virginia, Kentucky, etc. It may snow in those states a lot, or perhaps some years it may barely snow. If you invest in the equipment and labor and it doesn't snow, you are in serious trouble. Although I do not have much expertise with snow removal, one observation is that it's safer when you know you are going to have a higher demand for your services such is the case in Minnesota, Wisconsin, etc.

Alex Kirby is the owner of Trifecta Landscaping in Columbia, South Carolina. On episode #545 of the Green Industry Podcast, I asked him how he manages this winter employee dilemma. His answer was somewhat surprising, "January and February, eight weeks, we are slow. But what I tell guys and this is why I preach the no debt thing so hard. If you don't have debt and you don't have all these payments coming out of your bank account. As long as you are able to break even or make a slight profit for those eight weeks, who cares! If that's going to keep your team in line and you don't have to re-train anybody and your employees can take sort of a staycation. They can work fewer hours and enjoy some time with their family for eight weeks, more than they are used to, that is a win-win for everybody."

With energetic passion, Alex continued on to explain, "It's okay to have two months where you are preparing for the grind of the ten months. To me, it's like spring training in a baseball. We use January and February as a recalibrate, reconnect, refocus, reenergize. So let's not worry too much about slaying the profit margins for those months because we know it's going to be an uphill climb. We don't have snow here in South Carolina, so that's the #1 thing I tell people, throw that out the door. Customers typically run out of all their money from

Christmas so they are not going to do anything in January. And at the end of February, we might start with some spring cleanups and stuff like that. But, that's my answer. If you don't have debt, then does it really matter as long as you do the analysis on break even. What is my break-even number? What's my slight profit 10% or whatever? And give the employees who have been working so diligently for you that opportunity to work as much or as little as they want."

Alex's opinion is unique as he lives in South Carolina and has a large team. For guys who are solo though, the Johnny Mow save up money plan is a great way to go. And even if you saved up enough money for the winter instead of sitting on the couch all day it can be a good idea to work another side hustle in the winter or work on your passion project.

#92 - Having a Side Hustle

As we continue to explore making the most of the offseason it's necessary to note that it's okay to have a part-time job. Entrepreneurship has been idolized in our culture. As if working a job as an employee is somehow toxic and wrong. The truth is having a job can be a big blessing even if you own a lawn care or landscaping business. If it's too cold to work outside and there is not much demand for your services in the winter months, do not be ashamed to get a part-time job. If you do, be honest with your employer about the weeks you are available to work.

My friend Naylor Taliaferro has worked both as a UPS helper during the holidays and at an Amazon distribution center. I have other friends who own lawn and landscape businesses that have worked doing Uber Eats, DoorDash, serving at restaurants, big box stores, and other various jobs during the winter to bring in some revenue. Personally, I am very grateful for the years I was able to increase my hours working at a radio station in the winter months.

#93 - Spend Lots of Time with Family

The offseason can be an incredible time of the year to load up on quality time with family. I have some friends who play and coach in the NFL. Their season is intense especially if they make the playoffs and a Super Bowl run. It's a few months of long hours and quality time with family is sacrificed during the season. However, in the offseason, they load up with quality family time. The ebbs and flows of our season are similar to the NFL. Whereas their season and demand for their time are intense September - December that is typically how the spring rush is in the lawn and landscape industry. You already know in advance what is required during the spring rush. Therefore, with intentionality and a good financial plan, the offseason can be an incredible time to spend extra time with loved ones. As we mentioned with Andy Mulder's fine example of course we want to also stay on top of quality time during the regular season as well, but in the offseason be focused to make the most of the opportunity to lavish time on family.

#94 - Go On Vacation!

Very early in my lawn and landscaping career, I got into a very bad situation of becoming a rat in a wheel. My prices were too low and I had overcommitted to weekly lawn care maintenance commitments. Therefore going on vacation was next to impossible in those early days. And when I did get away for a short weekend trip it was usually stressful leading up to the vacation during and of course when I got back. And that my friend, is absolutely no way to live life.

What I learned was that if you are going to have a high-volume lawn maintenance company you definitely need to build it in a way that you as the owner can step away and your business can run without you. And if you do choose to be solo and proud then you need to consider and calculate how you are going to take vacations. If solo, one option is to load up and take multiple vacations during the offseason. Or another option is to focus more on landscape enhancements so that your schedule is not stretched thin with weekly recurring lawn maintenance. But if you are solo and do have lots of weekly lawn maintenance and want to go on vacation during the season then just communicate in advance with your customers about your plans. If your customers know, like, and trust you they should be understanding. Many companies take the week of the Equip Exposition in October off. Just email your customers in advance and let them know there is a business event your team is traveling to. Or if it's a beach trip for your anniversary, simply let them know the time you will be away and that you will take care of things when you get back. I deeply regret the years I ran around like a rat in the wheel and neglected vacations. The reason was my business was unorganized and I did not have the proper systems and people in place.

Depending on the variables in your situation, figure out a way in advance of how you can get away and enjoy traveling and vacation. I say all that though to emphasize that the winter is a golden opportunity for vacations. Although a spontaneous trip every now and again may be fun, planning ahead as a business leader is necessary. If you have the margin financially consider how you can enjoy some vacations in the offseason.

#95 - Get In Shape

The extra time in the offseason gives us many opportunities. One of those to consider is to get in better shape! Hopefully, during peak season you have discovered a rhythm to help you do some daily exercise or training other than the natural workout in the field. But, I get it, sometimes it's hard to find the time to exercise and pump some iron.

The ample time in the winter months though can be a great reset and improve our diet and get some workouts in. The more optimal our health is likely the better we will think and perform as business leaders. Therefore, make the most of winter and enjoy some time working out and improving your health and well-being.

#96 - Set New Goals

Here in the United States, the heart of our off-season is January and it just so happens to be the fresh start of a new year. What a great time to recalibrate and set some new goals for the year. The more specific and measurable you can set the goals, the more likely you are to get traction on achieving them. And write down your goals! I started doing this in college and it has helped transform my life. We actually have a goal tracker and journal that can help guide you through the process of writing down your goals. It's called *The Diligent Shall Prosper* and is available as a hardcover on Amazon.

13

Build to Sell

#97 - Build to Sell

In episode #582 of the Green Industry Podcast Kory Ballard shares some valuable insights about selling a lawn care business. Kory started his business as a teenager and in 2021 sold it. Along the journey, he learned a lot about the best ways to grow and sell your lawn care business. I would highly recommend listening to his wisdom from when he shared the story and his observations during that interview.

My takeaway after interviewing Kory on the topic is that the cleaner your books are the better. Someone who is interested in purchasing your business is going to want to know the plain truth about your financial history. By keeping things honest and clean throughout the history of your company the more valuable your business becomes at the point of sale. Additionally, keep your customer's information and work history organized. Someone interested in buying your company is not just buying the equipment and current customers, but they are also buying data. Imagine yourself as a data collection company in a sense. Those email addresses, phone numbers, and customers' work detail history have value. The new company that will be buying your company cares a lot about that data as it will help them with marketing and future revenues. In retrospect, keep your books squeaky clean and keep an organized database of your customer's work history and accurate contact information.

#98 - Name Your Business Carefully

The name of your business is significant. A good name will help market your business and it can also increase the amount someone pays for your company if you decide to sell it. For example, what business do you think will be sold for more money, Rick's Quality Lawn Care or Duluth Landscaping? The correct answer is Duluth Landscaping. The new owners can seamlessly make the transition and keep things rolling. However, Rick's Quality Landscaping is centered around Rick. After the business is sold since Rick is gone it could cause attrition.

A rule of thumb when naming your business is to be mindful that one day you might sell the business and also try to explain as much as you can about the business in the name. For example with Duluth Landscaping, it explains both what we do, landscaping, and what area the business serves, Duluth, GA in this example.

#99 - Consider a Business Broker When Selling

In some situations, a larger landscaping company may reach out to you and make an offer to buy your business. If you are interested in selling and it's a good deal, I would recommend hiring a reputable attorney. They can help you with the sale of your business and make sure it's done correctly. However, if you are considering possibly selling your business but do not have a serious buyer lined up, then you may want to search for a reputable business broker in your area with experience selling lawn and landscaping businesses. Although you will need to compensate them quite a bit, they may be able to help you find a buyer and sell your business for a lot more than you could sell it for alone.

14

Iron Sharpens Iron

#100 - Plug Into Your Local Community

There is an ancient saying that if you want to go fast, go alone, but if you want to go far go together. Unless you live in Timbuktu, there is likely a local lawn and landscape community in your area. There may be a bad apple here or there, but it's reasonable that there are others just like you in the area trying to build a profitable lawn and landscape business. Becoming friends with these folks can benefit both of you. Having friends in the industry in your local market can be helpful. As I previously mentioned, look into your local county extension office and find out what opportunities they offer. You can expect to meet like-minded business leaders at those training sessions with who you can network and help one another out.

#101 - Plug Into the Online Community

There is a growing vibrant online lawn and landscape community full of business leaders trying to take their businesses to the next level. Nowadays there are many quality podcasts that you can listen to and learn from. Brian Fullerton hosts the Fullerton Unfiltered Podcast, Caleb Auman has the Kid Contractor Podcast, Naylor Taliaferro hosts the LCR Media Podcast and Mike Pletz hosts the How to Hardscape Podcast just to name a few. These shows are full of knowledge and motivation to help you grow your business. There is also lawn and landscape content and community on YouTube and Instagram. Get in where you fit in and elevate your life and business with others who are trying to win too.

Something else that is unique about this community is how many ways people have utilized a lawn and landscape business to enhance their lives. Some like Kory Ballard have built huge lawn and snow companies with tens of millions in revenue. Others like Alex Kirby have built million-dollar businesses with 20+ employees. Then you have the

Caleb Auman's of the world with 2-3 crews doing around one million dollars per year. Then, there are others like Naylor Taliaferro keeping it more simple with one crew at incredible efficiency. Of course, there is Johnny Mow, solo and proud, working alone but crushing it financially.

Then there are the weekend warriors, folks like Mitchell's Lawn Care who have a profitable lawn business as a side hustle. Mitchell has a full-time career as a North Carolina State Trooper but enjoys extra income and doing work he loves with his part-time lawn business. And last but not least there are just homeowners who love taking care of their lawns that are a part of our lawn care community. I recently met the Lawn Tools from Arkansas. They are brothers who actually built a few golf holes in their backyard and share content across social media of their lawn care adventures. Whether you are looking for content about how to have a lush green yard (check out Allyn Hane, The Lawn Care Nut) or you are searching for pro tips to run a profitable operation, the online lawn care community is here to help.

Thank you for taking the time to read this book. Honestly, we could have done 201 Proven Ways To Increase Efficiency and Make More Money In Lawn Care. I'm just warming up, but we do have hundreds of podcast episodes so if you want more business insights about successfully growing your business check out the Green Industry Podcast. And for more resources and training programs check out our website

https://greenindustrypodcast.com/

Acknowledgments

I want to express my gratitude to Mr. Producer, who is both my podcast producer and friend. Not only did he help proofread and edit this book, but he also agreed to narrate the audio version which is available on Audible. He performs a valuable service for our community by bringing a professional sound to many of the podcasts I mentioned earlier. To connect with him for professional audio and voice services you can send him a direct message on Instagram @MrProducerUSA.

The entertaining story of how Paul Jamison went from launching his landscaping business out of the trunk of a rusty 1997 Honda Accord to now serving high profile, celebrity customers such as professional sports athletes and coaches is inspiring. Paul will have you on the edge of your seat as he humorously shares his journey of what he learned in the school of experience and on the job training.

What Can You Do to Immediately Boost Your Lawn Care or Landscaping Business Profits?

Running a landscaping business is not like running any other kind of company. You don't need generic business advice. You need proven tactics and strategies from people who know exactly what kinds of challenges you're facing.

That's why Paul Jamison's *Best Business Practices for Landscapers* is an essential read for anyone even thinking about starting a lawn care or landscaping company.

Jamison is best known as the host of the *Green Industry Podcast*, where he interviews the most successful landscaper entrepreneurs about their journeys. He is also the author of the highly successful book *Cut the Grass and Make That Cash*.

This book is full of powerful insights you won't find anywhere else. If you read this book and apply all of the lessons, you will watch your landscaping business profits skyrocket.

Achieve the goals and dreams you have for you and your business faster with the aid of this thought-provoking goal tracker and journal.

It is a time-tested principle that you can effectively propel your life forward by:

- Writing Down Your Goals
- Making Plans To Achieve Them
- Working On Them Every Single Day

This practice has changed Paul Jamison's life and the lives of millions of other people. It will change yours as well!

Start your adventure to new heights through the power of gratitude, a daily proverb from the wisest man to ever live, and recording your thoughts and observations in this journal. Develop the habits of diligent people that lead to prosperity and crushing your goals!

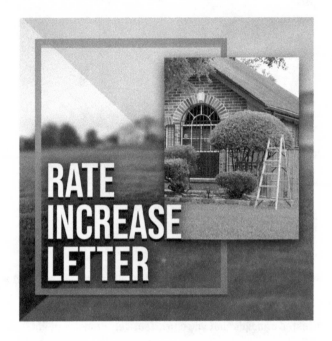

The rate increase letter is a plug and play template to help you clearly and concisely communicate with your customers that you are raising your rates.

Available at GreenIndustryPodcast.com

The Pricing Matrix is a spreadsheet that gives you the opportunity to know what you are earning per man hour for each customer. You simply input what price you charged the customer, what time your crew started the maintenance and what time they finished the main-tenance and how many employees were on the job. The pricing matrix algorithm will then calculate the actual man hours as well as what you earned per man hour on the job.

CPSIA information can be obtained
at www.ICGtesting.com
Printed in the USA
LVHW100200110422
715864LV00018B/127